IAIN SODEN

First published 2013

Amberley Publishing
The Hill, Stroud
Gloucestershire, GL5 4EP

www.amberley-books.com

British Library Cataloguing in Publication Data.
A catalogue record for this book is available from the British Library.

ISBN 978 1 84868 833 9
Ebook ISBN 978 1 4456 1203 4

Typesetting and Origination by Amberley Publishing.
Printed in the UK.

CONTENTS

ACKNOWLEDGEMENTS

The research that has gone into this book since 2008 in a challenging economic climate would not have been possible without the dedication and the expert knowledge of the staff of numerous libraries and record offices across England, France and Belgium. In particular I am indebted to the staff of the British Library and to the Municipal Archives in Bruges for their guidance and their ability to source the necessary documentation without fuss or bother – and put up with me.

I am grateful to the National Portrait Gallery, London, for their permission to publish images from their fantastic collections. I am also grateful to the staff of Northamptonshire Libraries and Northamptonshire Record Society, together with Birmingham Reference Library, who put up with me as they were preparing to move their entire reserve stack into storage while a new library was built. It is to all libraries' credit that they continue to do their jobs without fuss or furore, to the public at least, as they strive to work under ever stricter financial constraints. The staff of three-dozen castles and stately homes, and countless bemused farmers, have humoured me in my searches across wind-eroded earthworks and landscapes of exile.

I am indebted to the following for their support throughout or at notable moments in the research and writing of this book:

To Rachel Swallow goes my heartfelt gratitude. To Sallie Gee goes my admiration for her contribution to 'Mary, Queen of Scots' and for her comments on my text. To Amir Bassir go my thanks for his expert line-drawings. To both he and Tony Walsh go my thanks for their digital scans of my older slides and prints. To my old friend Joe Prentice goes my gratitude for giving me access to his antiquarian library. To my Father, for his photographic advice (it shows where I took it), and to my Mother for being his rock. Lastly, thanks to Annette, my wife, for travelling this road with me unswervingly and never ceasing to love and astound me through it all.

There is no small part of each of you in this book and it is to you all that I affectionately dedicate the book and the effort it has entailed.

Northamptonshire
August 2012

INTRODUCTION

This is a book about hope. It is the hope of privileged royalty and nobility faced with the removal of every last relevance of that privilege, along with any apparent promise of it ever being regained.

Using case studies between 1192 and 1660, this book looks at the mechanics of medieval Europe's royal houses (principally those of England and France, by choice) to take and keep indefinitely prisoners and hostages, and to drive their opposite numbers into exile to preserve a chosen status quo, both in war and peace. To each generation it was a pure construct, a society within a society, with its own economy, its own etiquette, its hosts, and its unwilling guests trying daily to acquit themselves in a manner their homelands, their families and their God would expect. In some cases they took with them only what they could carry, sometimes little more than the clothes on their backs. In other cases they tried to live sumptuously, but out of sight and increasingly irrelevant in their homeland. It called for perseverance, fortitude and extreme patience in the face of extreme boredom. It was soul-destroying, frustrating and poverty-inducing and, occasionally, there was no happy ending. For this story, the rights and wrongs of a cause, imprisonment on matters of conscience, are not a concern. In a medieval world not generally given to ideals and political ethics, conscience was largely dictated by Church and State and there was little else in the way of ideas that ever coalesced to seriously contradict these until the gathering storm of the Reformation poured out across the Continent.

The world in which we live today has, on the surface, changed beyond all recognition from that which our medieval forebears knew. However, people and regimes do not change. Their hopes, their aspirations, their fears and their sorrows spring from the same wells and have similar roots: love of family, companionship, friendship, faith in a god, security and a long and happy life.

The international news when I was a young student was dominated by firstly the Iranian Revolution and then the bitter civil war in Lebanon. I was fascinated by the rapidly fading glory of the Peacock throne, with a still much-respected but increasingly ailing Shah of Iran, Mohamed Reza Pahlavi, going into European exile, followed by the incredible fortitude of Terry Waite, Brian Keenan and John McCarthy, chained to radiators in their separate Lebanese confinements, the boredom, if not the fear, only eventually lightened a little by the sounds of home in the BBC World Service. Their stories were played out (largely unbeknown to them) in ordinary living rooms across the world while they sat powerless to guide their own futures as events ran away with them. Their powerlessness struck me. So did their stoicism, fortitude and eventually, upon their release, their humanity. How would I react in similar circumstances? Would I have the strength of character? Is it a case of the more I have and the more I expect, the less I can exist without it?

Perhaps I got closest to the feelings of powerlessness when I wrote my previous book, *Ranulf de Blondeville: The First English Hero*.[1] Here was a man born into privilege who in 1204, along with his Breton wife, lost his entire Norman patrimony and was forced to start again in England without his friends, his associates, and half his lands, apparently prevented from ever returning to his homeland. In an age of war and chivalry, he returned in triumph as an ageing knight of immense renown, already the saviour of England and a famous crusader, to successfully claim at least some of it back. He never gave up hope. He showed gratitude to his friends, and grace under pressure.

We all perhaps spend periods in self-imposed exile or incarcerated in mental prisons of our own making. Our thoughts, our actions like some Prometheus, our beliefs, our perceptions, whether genuinely held or misguided, have the potential to leave us bound in our own personal prison or exiled from our peers. There is, therefore, a light we hold up in common with real, physical prisoners and exiles, the flame of hope that we all have for freedom, to lighten even the darkest Robben Island cell. It is a thread to negotiate a darkened labyrinth, like Theseus, physically freeing hostages who are terrified and powerless to help themselves, or a hope in a saviour, such as Jesus Christ, who in his own words came 'to proclaim freedom for the prisoners'.[2]

The medieval world was no different from our own in this respect. Prisoners need hope of release. Hostages need a hope of parole. Exiles need a mental glimpse of the green, green grass of home. In some ways there is little to choose between the homesickness of the Duke of Orleans and the Duke and Duchess of Windsor after Edward VIII's abdication, creating a new world, a home from home. Likewise the cultured Shah of Iran may perhaps be broadly compared with Edward IV, except for the eventual differing outcomes. Edward IV returned to raise an army and mounted a successful coup; the Shah died in exile.

For a royal exile or prisoner in the medieval world, the winner more than ever told the story. Deposed or disenfranchised exiles who did not return, and prisoners who went to the block, were painted as villains (such as Charles I). It is no different today. Those who returned in a victorious coup were forever saviours (such as Charles II). More than ever, it depends upon hindsight's standpoint.

In 2012, Aung San Suu Kyi was finally released to her adoring people in Myanmar and all across the world. The flame still burns while there are those who choose to keep it alight.

1

A CAGED LION

RICHARD I IN AUSTRIA & GERMANY (1192–94)

Universally known as the Lionheart for his prowess in battle, Richard's two years at the Third Crusade were over and done with by the middle of 1192. However, his return to Normandy and England was to prove difficult and drawn-out.

He may have been able to avoid the unpleasantness of his return journey had he, in 1191, avoided a slight to one of his allies on crusade. There, stood in the line next to the contingent of Leopold, Duke of Austria, during a siege, a horse shied and the duke's standard dropped to the ground. Instead of its immediate retrieval, some of Richard's retainers' skittish horses trampled it into the dust. Unapologetic, Richard made light of it. The duke would never forget it and his early return from the Holy Land gave him time and space to nurse this slight to his dignity.

As with many crusaders' journeys, the course to and from the Holy Land was part by land, part by sea. Richard's own crusade petered out at Jaffa in early August 1192. He had managed to relieve the town from siege by Saladin and open negotiations for a truce. Both Richard and the Muslim commander, Saladin, took the opportunity to try to reinforce at this time, Saladin welcoming an army under his brother Saphadin from Egypt. Richard summoned French forces at Caesarea but they refused to come, their own king, Philip Augustus, having long departed for home. Nevertheless, when truce negotiations with Saladin broke down (Saladin knowing he had the upper hand), Richard indicated his intention to remain in Palestine, perhaps now something of an empty threat as his forces were clearly no longer united.

At about the middle of the month Richard fell ill at Jaffa. It is unclear what afflicted him but his army had been badly affected by dysentery for some time. Saladin continued to redeploy his increasing forces, taking advantage of Richard's inactivity. Truce negotiations resumed, probably under the Bishop of Salisbury, and a three-year truce was signed on 2 September. Perhaps in order to seal the truce, Saphadin, who had once been tipped as a prospective husband for Richard's sister, presented Richard with three magnificent Arab horses, a generous gift which the king accepted.[1] Richard then moved from Jaffa to Haifa where the air and water were better for his health and, unable for the present to meet his obligations, handed over army command to a trusted deputy. Clearly buoyed by Richard's low state, Saladin, along with Saphadin, moved his camp on 13 September to Jerusalem, their position now unassailable.

Later in the month Richard moved on to Acre, ransoming prisoners from Muslim hands, in a move clearly preparatory to taking his leave. He packed his wife, Queen Berengaria, and other royals off from Acre by the end of the month and made arrangements for his own departure, which eventually took place on 9 October.

Although his journey was meant to be to Marseille in the first instance, he diverted via Corfu, then a friendly crusader port owned by Constantinople, then hopped over via the normal sea lanes to Italy amid Adriatic storms. His progress was noted off Brindisi (Italy) before he was blown horribly off course eastwards to Dubrovnik (in Croatia, and formerly called *Ragusa*), where pirates forced him to put in. There he remained for a while, the pious Richard taking the opportunity to found the cathedral. When he eventually set out again, his passage along the eastern coast continued to be dogged by stormy weather and he only disembarked with difficulty between Venice and Aquileia, his ship being apparently shipwrecked (perhaps an exaggeration by the dramatic William of Newburgh) or at least forced to beach. At least five others travelled with him. All managed to secure horses, if they had not made landfall with their own mounts, perhaps three distinctive Arabs among them.

The Holy Roman Emperor, Henry VI, meanwhile, had got wind of Richard's difficult sea passage and had put the coast on alert. Richard was clearly out of favour and, if found, was to be arrested. Faced with the near-impassable winter barrier of the Alps to the north-west, the party struck north for the Danube, Eastern Europe's greatest highway, as fast as their horses could carry them. Six knights in the group were captured as Richard himself gave the Emperor's agent (Count Mainhard of Goritz) the slip at Friesach (just north of Klagenfurt, Austria) with the help of an expatriate Norman knight who gave him fresh horses.[2] He then tried to pick his way through the still-simmering Leopold of Austria's territory.

Since the Emperor now knew the rough composition of the English party, they split up and Richard, deliberately dressing down, together with a single knight and a young guide and interpreter, rode north until he reached the southern outskirts of Vienna, having covered over 260 miles in seven days and nights of hard riding. Exhausted, they went into hiding in a nearby village but were discovered after three days and arrested by ducal troops on 20 December 1192.[3] Only three days later he was taken under guard from Vienna up the Danube to Leopold's castle at Dürnstein, a fortress-eyrie which commanded the north bank of the Danube.[4]

Here he would be suitably out of the way while the Austrian court celebrated Christmas. William of Newburgh says dramatically that Richard was put 'in chains' although this may be sensationalising the story (again).[5] Another, perhaps shying away from such extremes, says that he was, if not actually in chains, the victim of some rough treatment and poor conditions.[6] This is perhaps closer to the truth, since up until the late medieval period Germanic prisons in particular gained a fearsome reputation in this manner.[7] Word of Richard's arrest was sent to the Emperor Henry VI, which he received within eight days and which he quickly shared gleefully in a letter to his ally Philip Augustus of France. To prevent anyone rallying around the English king, the Duke of Austria allowed, on payment of a fine, the safe passage of numerous other crusaders through his territory.

Even today the castle at Dürnstein lies perched on a bluff above the eponymous village where the Danube bends noticeably about 30 miles upstream, west of Vienna. In the twelfth century this represented about two days' sailing by barge against the considerable current. Draught horses along the banks and oars could also be used against the flow if the wind alone was insufficient or unfavourable. Dürnstein was an imposing introduction to Richard's captor and even today it remains his best-known, if little-visited prison. It has lost none of its power, although a ruin. The village below, which stretches down to the river-bank, still thrives and would once have been the location of a river ferry and landing stage. The castle provided a customs post for the city of Vienna downstream and a boom, or chain, could be strung across the navigable channels to force traffic to stop, tie up and pay their dues. It was the kind of arrangement Richard would later remember when building Château Gaillard above the River Seine.

Hardly had Richard been incarcerated in Dürnstein, than he was moved to a hurried informal presentation by the duke before the Emperor, who that year held his Christmas court at Regensburg (formerly called *Ratisbon*), a journey up the Danube by barge, against the current, of some 190 miles. He was then moved back to Dürnstein for a short while.

Less than two months after his capture, word of Richard's fate was being discussed in England. The Archbishop of Rouen arranged with his fellow Bishop of Durham to convene a meeting to discuss the situation at Oxford on 28 February.

An England already divided by Richard's prolonged absence now increasingly began to fragment, fomented by Richard's avaricious younger brother, Prince John. He argued that his brother was in fact dead (although he knew the truth from the outset).[8] He was now trying to do business with the French king, who talked diplomacy but pressed hard with his military might.

Although the Oxford meeting sent the Bishop of Bath (distantly related to the Holy Roman Emperor) to begin negotiations for Richard's release, the king himself had also to be actually found. Sadly the romantic story of a wandering minstrel, Blondel, stumbling upon the king at Dürnstein is a Victorian myth. In fact the council of churchmen sent the abbots of Boxley and Robertsbridge (Sussex) to Germany to find the king, who was travelling with the Imperial court as their prisoner.[9] Richard was being taken west and north, up the Danube and then along the valley of the Wörnitz and what is today known as the Romantische Straße, a principal salt route through Nördlingen and Rothenburg. Following a trail of consistent local gossip and rumour, and with a limit to the number of winter roads the court could take between two places, a captive king in transit was probably not that difficult to track down. The two abbots were said to have searched high and low across Germany, a blatant exaggeration – it took them only three weeks from Oxford, even in late winter. They located him in what is now the Franken region of northern Bavaria at Ochsenfurt am Main, about 10 miles from Würzburg, the principal crossing of the Main, where they secured a meeting with him on Palm Sunday (21 March) 1193.[10]

Thus diplomatic contact with England was now restored by his discovery and Richard was no longer just a prisoner. He could now expect to attain some kind of recognition. Certainly the public knowledge of his safety and whereabouts, if not yet any recovered status, may have played a part in Philip Augustus of France taking fright in April and abandoning a siege of Rouen, at the heart of Richard's Norman dominions. Ignominiously, he withdrew in such haste he was forced to burn his own siege equipment, which he had had in position encircling the city.

Expecting by now an audience with the Emperor, Richard was deliberately kept waiting at Ochsenfurt, notably for three days, a specific period which was probably deliberate since it was a biblically inspired period of spiritual preparation. He was, after all, about to be given an audience by the holy and anointed head of the Church's protector on earth, the Roman Empire, in whose hands his fate and that of his kingdom lay. He was said to have spent the time in a dignified and prudent manner,[11] despite some anger at his brother's scheming, of which he was now informed. Three days was enough too to leave him in no uncertainty that the Emperor was in a class of his own.

At the audience with Henry, Richard's status was acknowledged and his considerable ransom and the political terms of his release, under deliberation since mid-February, were set out for negotiation. Richard was now formally handed over by Leopold as captor to Henry as jailer. For a duke to have continued to hold a king would have been to incur greater displeasure from the Church, already stirred up at the unwelcome violation of (so well known) a crusader's right to be left unmolested.

Within a couple of weeks Richard had gathered around him a small court in exile, advised by Hubert, Bishop of Salisbury, and a few trusted knights who had begun to visit him, word having reached them on their own journey home from the crusade. He was able to begin an exchange of diplomatic letters, although these were no doubt opened by the Emperor's own secretaries. Richard wrote to his mother, the redoubtable Eleanor of Aquitaine, whose power-broking kept something approximating to balance across Western Europe. Richard made every effort to exert some influence at home through a series of specific preferments to the Church in England, whose power might hold John in check. Notably, in order to avoid censorship or the interception of letters, the crux of his dealings was by word of mouth alone, Eleanor being encouraged in writing to trust what his envoy would say to her.[12] He would also be able to publish the proposed itinerary of the Holy Roman court, since in the weeks it would take for letters to go, be acted upon and replies sent, Richard might well have moved on. And indeed he had – to Speyer on the Rhine towards the end of March.

After less than a month in Speyer, Richard moved up the Rhine to the safe custody of the strong castle of Trifels, where the imperial insignia were kept, in a move which was probably designed to sharpen the departing envoys' focus on his plight. Here indeed the bishop and his envoys took their leave, to cross Alsace, Burgundy and the Kingdom of France to England, a journey which took them nineteen days as the weather began to improve with spring. At the intervention of his chancellor, who arrived in early April and was shocked at his king's new quarters, Richard was subsequently moved to nearby Haguenau where the Roman court was sitting. He then wrote again to England, and the broad terms of his ransom (still being hammered out) were set out for English benefit. The chancellor set off with the second diplomatic bag, and Richard began a relatively settled period, moving from Haguenau in late May to Worms, where he would remain for the summer, regularly writing to England, sending a diplomatic bag back with each group of visitors he received. In each case he could only say so much, the nub of his policy in exile, which was centred upon the election of new Church leaders as his statesmen, being communicated by word of mouth alone via the nominated envoy. His correspondents were told to put their confidence in what each envoy would tell them personally. He clearly could not trust his plans to writing, lest they be read by agents at every turn.

At the end of June the ransom terms were finally settled even though arrangements for its collection had been in train in England as early as April. A hundred thousand silver marks was a king's ransom indeed. Many hostages would be needed since it would be unlikely that such a sum could be raised quickly (at least not if John had anything to do with it). The clock was now ticking and the Emperor knew it. Seeing that matters were now no longer fully in his control, he wrote to Prince John and informed him, 'The devil is loose.' Although still far removed from his place of exile, Richard's counsellors now began to deal once more with Philip Augustus of France in Richard's name, his court now functioning, albeit from a distance and informed only irregularly of events in a dysfunctional England and a restive Normandy. Richard's settled summer at Worms, dominated by a magnificent new Cathedral of St Peter, gave rise to a growing postbag and he was able to give time to issuing charters for churches and monasteries which were out of the public eye. It was a parochial side of Richard which saw him giving time and thought to ordinary town life in England, half a continent away. He wrote twice in late May and early June as this settled existence gave rise to an ability to take his time over decision making. Henry was careful not to stir up his captive's anger and, while calling him 'devil' to John, then described him as 'our most dear and illustrious King Richard' in a letter to the nobles of England.[13] Nevertheless he urged them to comply with the ransom demand, the implications if they did not being left unspoken.

A trusted group of churchmen and loyal nobles in England were given the responsibility of overseeing the collection of the ransom and Richard could do little more than wait.

It was only with the annual preparations for the Emperor's Christmas court that Richard was moved back up the Rhine late in November to Speyer once more, into more commodious surroundings. The surroundings may have been better, but it was in the wrong direction, upstream – away from England.

Henry, possibly as part of a plan to ingratiate himself now that it was becoming clear that his custody of Richard could not last forever, offered him the Kingdom of Arles (Provence) with dependencies in Burgundy and across the Rhone up to the Alps, even though (ironically) he himself had little claim over it.[14] It was probably in response to early mention of this that Richard sent for his mother, Eleanor, who, as Dowager Duchess of Aquitaine, knew well the politics of the many kingdoms, duchies and counties which made up what is now France. In fact she could be said to have written the manual. In preparation for the longed-for day, Richard had already sent for his admiral, Alan Trenchemer, who, amid resurgent royal authority, would facilitate his Channel crossing following his release.[15]

In a letter to the English barons Henry set a date for Richard's release, 17 January 1194, with his Coronation as King of Arles due to take place, probably at Worms, on 24 January. The event had to be delayed, however, as Henry seems to have had second thoughts about his gift and the date of Richard's release. Winter weather may have played a part, as Richard did in fact not leave Speyer for Worms again (another boat journey down the Rhine) until at least 22 January. He was still not a free man. His continued captivity was causing unrest, however. It was frowned upon by the Church and Richard had made many noble German friends during his captivity who were beginning to agitate for him. Henry cast the dice one last time, digging up old trumped-up murder charges for an incident in the Holy Land. Against clearly false witness, the German bishops, backed by Richard's new German allies, stood up to Henry and urged him to meet his obligations. [16]

Further down the Rhine at Mainz, Richard was finally joined by his mother, Eleanor, the Archbishop of Rouen and the Bishop of Bath, together with those who would stand hostage for Richard until the ransom was fully paid. There on 2 February 1194, on the advice of his mother, Eleanor of Aquitaine, Richard gave England up to the Emperor and agreed to pay him homage as his liege lord for England and an annual payment of £5,000. Faced with the prospect of the Kingdom of England to add to his Empire and compromised by his own restive bishops and nobility, Henry relented and on 4 March at Mainz, Richard was set free after one year, six months and three days. The toughest of English hearts melted and the assembled company was said to have wept for joy.[17]

Accompanied by armed German guards, to 'protect' the group (and escort back to Germany more hostages), the king set out by barge north down the Rhine to Cologne, where the ever pious Richard heard Mass for his safe release. Setting foot on soil again, the Archbishop of Cologne then travelled west with him as far as Antwerp but here they found a hostile fleet lay in wait, John having been tipped off about Richard's itinerary. Alan Trenchemer had been dodging them for some time. In order to give them the slip Richard swapped boats and slept on different vessels while at Antwerp, one of them a huge and beautiful ship sent from Rye, but he was unable to put out and was forced to head south.[18] It took him four days to get from Antwerp to Flanders and the Zwin estuary (the old port of Bruges), where, due to Prince John's continued watch on the coast, his departure was further delayed for another five days. On the sixth day they were able to put out on the dawn tide, slipping past the coastal watch, and after little more than a day and a night's sailing they made landfall on the afternoon of 13 March 1194 at Sandwich in Kent. Stopping briefly at Canterbury, Richard moved to London to begin the process of securing his kingdom once more. Once there, his German guards were astounded at what they saw. Had they known the wealth they saw in England's capital, they said they would have increased the ransom.

Within the year Richard's captor, the Duke of Austria, was dead from a smashed leg he suffered in a riding accident.[19] Henry, Richard's jailer, could not make the ransom stick and he released the hostages, renouncing too his claim to England at the insistence of Rome.

The Lionheart went straight back into battle at Nottingham, doing what he did best. There the rebellious castle, already under siege for a month in his absence, could barely believe it was the king who now stood at their gates.[20] A frontal attack and the use of Greek fire was all the persuasion they needed to capitulate. On 17 April Richard was crowned again in a special ceremony at Winchester, his authority restored. With England quickly secured, he spent the next five years trying to undo the damage his brother, John, and Philip Augustus of France had done to Normandy in his absence. He also built a riverside castle at Château Gaillard whose chosen location commanding the Seine was probably very much influenced by what he had seen and experienced at Dürnstein on the Danube.

2

A KING'S RANSOM

JEAN II OF FRANCE IN ENGLAND (1356–60, 1363–64)

The Battle of Poitiers on Monday 19 September 1356 was the kind of military victory most countries at war dream of but win usually once in a generation or less. Like Crècy before (1346) and Agincourt after (1415), Poitiers was a high-water mark for England in the grinding attrition which characterised the Hundred Years' War. The English casualties were light compared with the bloodletting on the French side, blood which flowed like wine among the Poitevin vines where their youth was cut down in droves. The English chronicler John Capgrave (1393–1464) is perhaps among the least jingoistic of recorders but his information was gleaned from the self-satisfied many that had been there:

> At the last ende of that yere he met with the French king fast be Peytris [Poitiers]. The prince had in his felauchip not passed III thousand; and the Kyng of Frans had IIII batayles. But for all that, the French fled, the kyng was take, and Philippe, his younger son, James Bourbon and XI erles, the bischop Senonensis [Sens], with other lordis and knytes to the noumbyr of too thousand. There were killed too dukes, XIX lordes and five thousand of men of armes, beside othir puple.[1]

It was ironic that the French king, Jean II, also known as Jean le Bon (John the Good), commanding in person, at the opening of the battle had flown the standard which bid his troops to take no English prisoners. Equally ironic then that he himself, surrounded and fighting like a lion, had been taken prisoner by half a dozen English and Gascon lords who from the outset all vied to be acknowledged as the one who captured a king, his ransom enough to make them all rich beyond their wildest dreams.[2]

As the French fled in disarray, leaving the flower of a generation dead on the field, so many were captured (more than 2,000) that, stripped of their weapons and armour, relieved of their valuable warhorses, large numbers were sent on their way merely on the promise that they would honour the chivalric code by raising an agreed ransom and paying up by Christmas.[3] A core, however, were held, because they represented the heart of the entire French royal court and its government. In one fell swoop France personified had been beheaded.[4]

Stunned by their own victory, the English held a banquet on the field at day's end at the behest of their commander Edward, the Black Prince. As Prince of Wales, Earl of Chester and Earl of Cornwall, Edward was the epitome of medieval chivalry and his victory at Poitiers ensured that a military reputation already fully formed now received its gilding. At the supper, he proceeded to serve in person the same French king who only hours before had sought his own death with no apparent hope of capture. Edward's singular chivalry and humility probably only served to make Jean uncomfortable, not least because he had himself been the author of the French Order of the Star, an equivalent to England's new Order of the Garter. Both were considered the foremost marks of chivalry among Europe's ruling elite at the time.

Alongside King Jean, the contemporary chroniclers relate a list of the noble prisoners, which merely serves to indicate how leaderless and powerless France became overnight.

There was the king's youngest son, Prince Philippe, aged just fifteen; Arnauld d'Audenham, the aged but highly respected Marshall of France; and the Count of Tancarville, Chamberlain of France. Other royals were taken, comprising the counts of Ponthieu, Longueville, Joigny and Eu, all closely related to Jean. The list of nobles also included the counts of Sancerre, Aubigny, Ventadour, Aussore and Vendôme. To these were added the lords d'Aubigny and Craonne and Sir Hugh de Chastillon. It also included the Bishop of Sens, and the Archbishop of Le Mans who was captured by the Earl of Warwick. No definitive list of the prisoners by name has ever been compiled and the roll call of the very valuable ones probably ran into hundreds.[5] Of course Jean's own closest retainers and servants had to go with him; they could not leave or abandon him in his hour of need so they went with him into captivity. It was in stark contrast to the Duke of Orleans and other of the king's sons, who had embarrassingly shown clean pairs of heels before they had even entered the battle.

In the company of their captors headed by the Black Prince, King Jean and his court made a rapid and (probably) embarrassed journey across English-held Gascony to Bordeaux, capital of England's dominions in France. It was a royal progress of sorts, unavoidable perhaps, not very stately, but still a potent showing-off to any who might waver, that their loyalty to England would always pay off. Here was the King of France, powerless. Here was France itself brought low. The rush was on to get the most valuable of human cargoes deep into English territory and carry the unbelievable news to King Edward III, back in England.

From La Roche on 20/21 September, they proceeded to Conté, Ruffec, Verteuil-sur-Charente and Mouton, and on to Rochefoucault on Sunday 25 September. On without more than a night's rest to Villebois-Lavalette, Saint Claye; over the Dronne on the 28th, the Lisle the next day, to the fabulously wealthy St Emilion and a night crossing of the Dordogne before entering Libourne and Bordeaux in triumph on Sunday 2 October [6] Word had gone ahead of them. The city's reception of the Black Prince and his prisoner was ecstatic.[7]

When the news reached England the bearer of the good tidings was handsomely rewarded, while at Westminster a group of English lords, breaking up after a meeting of the Royal Council, stayed on to party hard with the king for two days, incurring additional expenses that Edward III gladly paid in full.[8]

In addition to the valuable prisoners, the booty that was taken in the battle was considerable and this was divided up. The most notable is that which fell at the time, or by later arrangement, to the Black Prince himself and therefore crops up in his surviving records as values were settled and deals done. It included a magnificent silver ship, which was probably a table centrepiece (and a potent contemporary symbol of the ship of state, now very much aground), a crown and a star (his chivalric order).[9] Even his Bible was a battle trophy. Evidence also comes out of Edward's great chivalry, and possible compassion, since the same records also note his gift at the time of the battle of a captured black charger, given to an unnamed French prisoner, who had presumably lost his own or could not walk for his injuries.[10]

Throughout the winter the Black Prince and his court stayed in the area of Bordeaux, while Jean and his fellow captives were put up in the abbey of St André, one of the few buildings of sufficient size and comfort for the king. He would now have been joined by further servants and retainers thought indispensable for a king. In Bordeaux he entertained the local Anglo-Gascon nobility, who were probably both amused and overawed; he also met with Cardinal Talleyrand of Périgord, who had been trying to broker a peace of sorts throughout. Meanwhile news of Jean's capture raced north for England. It was finally reported to Edward III by John Cook, an inhabitant of Cherbourg, who was given 25 marks for this 'pleasing intelligence'; needing to separate fact from rumour, one of the prince's grooms later backed this up by presenting the French king's tunic and helmet as evidence. The news seems to have been the excuse for a party as a group of the Royal Council and government stayed on at Westminster to celebrate, running up a considerable parliamentary expenses bill which the king agreed to pay.[11]

The news also spread in other directions. In Rome, the Pope had been working to promote peace between England and France for some time, with little result. Back in May two cardinals, Talleyrand and Albano, the former with a long diplomatic pedigree, had been sent to the English and French courts to negotiate peace between the two countries.[12] Not least because he had himself been present at Poitiers where his shuttle diplomacy was said to have enabled the French army to grow in numbers to English disadvantage, and had subsequently met with Jean at Bordeaux, Talleyrand was not favoured by the English.[13] However, his presence meant the news of Jean's capture reached the Pope in early October, less than a month after the battle, probably among a flurry of letters asking for papal intervention, the cardinals' remit now being somewhat in need of new instructions. Letters dated early in December made provision for Roger Newmill, Papal Master Usher, to be sent to King Jean, who at that time was still in Bordeaux. The Pope also wrote to the Black Prince, asking him not to send one of his other prisoners, Charles of Arras, the Count of Longueville, to England. He was excused for the moment since papal pressure was not easily resisted without good cause. One must presume that the Pope had fully realised that King Jean was himself going to be sent to England and there was no point in arguing on that count.[14]

Arrangements were made for the return of Jean to England, although Gascon lords agitated for him to be retained there in Gascony. The prince's own retinue in Gascony amounted to 1,200 men and 400 horses, so preparations for embarkation, even for the English alone, were considerable.[15] They finally set sail at the beginning of May, landing at Plymouth on 5 May. The king accompanied the Black Prince, aboard a ship named the *Saint Mary*, manned with 100 marines, for which the prince paid a considerable sum for both the ship and its master. Disembarkation was probably unhurried as they found enough time in their itinerary to be entertained for three days at Exeter and new horses were bought locally for those nobles and knights whose own mounts had been killed or lost in the voyage.[16] They reached London on 14 May accompanied by the cardinals of Urgel and Albano and the prominent figure of Cardinal Talleyrand of Périgord. All three would stay for a year, along with their voracious and ostentatious courts.[17]

Contemporaries are agreed that the triumphal entry into London was a spectacle to behold, the French king in the lead on a great white thoroughbred, the Black Prince on a little black pony beside him, not in front, as his chivalric code dictated. Seemingly all of London turned out to see them. Thomas Walsingham, in particular, relates,

On 24 May [1357] the prince leading alongside him the King of France and the other captives crossed London Bridge and entered the city, and at about nine o'clock in the morning they turned towards Westminster; there such a multitude milled around them to see the spectacle, that due to the press of the crowd, they were unable to reach the Palace until gone midday.[18]

After his reception at the Palace of Westminster, Jean was taken to the relative luxury of the Savoy, a palace on the Strand then owned by the Duke of Lancaster but on land granted by the Crown to the Duke of Savoy, whose name it echoed. It might almost have been a small piece of home from home, if indeed Savoy had been part of the Kingdom of France, which at that time it was not. Although there can be little doubt that Jean was comfortable at the Savoy, concern seems to have grown about the French king's safety, or more likely the security of the Savoy (and with it England's investment in its royal hostage) since in September, Edward III engaged a troop of eighteen marines to watch the king from Edward's own royal barge, moored on the Thames nearby both day and night.[19]

In fact, if someone was planning to spring the French king from his velvet-lined cage that autumn, they would have had plenty of opportunity since, although he now began to gather around himself the semblance of a royal court once more, he was shuttled back and forth to Windsor and Eltham where he and the various noble members of his imprisoned court-in-exile were entertained by the king and queen, the Black Prince and the doughty dowager queen, Isabella. As widow of Edward II and herself French, she readily entertained on familiar terms the Marshall of France and Lord Aubigny over Christmas at her residence at Hertford Castle. The marshal in particular was a favourite of Isabella and he ate regularly as her guest throughout late 1357 and the first half of the following year, often accompanying King Jean and with numerous other members of the French court.[20] While Isabella's royal hospitality cannot be in doubt, many occasions were pure diplomatic manoeuvring; some in relation to a direct appeal to her from the Pope (Innocent VI) to intervene on Jean's behalf to petition for his release late in 1357,[21] others due to a personal interest in the fortunes of Charles the Bad, King of Navarre, whose own jailbreak from French captivity was reported to her on 16 November. Described as 'talented, enterprising but treacherous', and also in England's pay, he immediately went on the offensive in France and eventually took Paris while the Prince of Wales campaigned in Picardy and a leaderless France dithered.[22] Almost alone, Charles's efforts would scupper any hopes of a lasting peace treaty.

There is every indication that for the first part of his confinement, at least, Jean was very properly treated as the King of France he was. There was all deference paid to him, and those aspects due to him by divine right had barely to be asked for. In the next few years Edward III spent huge sums on sumptuous jewels in ostentatious settings for Jean, particularly rings set with diamonds and rubies. His own royal regalia was captured in the French camp at Poitiers or left behind in France, since he would not have worn such things in battle.[23] His liking for fine bespoke jewellery was to be a hallmark of his stay in England, both as gifts and as purchases of his own.

In fact, English expenses were huge in those early months, and not only for the French king. In mid-1357 Cardinal Albano arrived with his own court of 150, with 100 horses. Similar courts arrived with the two other cardinals and each were provided for in London, drawing in poultry from Kent and Sussex, and wheat, beans and oats from Lincolnshire, Cambridgeshire and Norfolk. The Bishop of Terouane arrived also with thirty horsemen, grooms, harness and trappings, all just to support the bishop who, along with the cardinals, was to take part in already protracted negotiations for Jean's release. Jean's own servants too now scoured the country gathering hay, oats, litter, meat, fish, corn and all the groceries needed for the Continental tastes of a court which seems to have numbered at least 100.[24] These papal emissaries were not empty-handed, however, and one brought a magnificent charger as a gift for Edward III, to smooth negotiations.

Still shuttling between the Savoy, Eltham and Windsor, much entertained by the English royal family and prominent nobles, King Jean spent some of these leisured days in sporting pursuits, in hunting and falconry, neither particular favourites of a man who normally apparently took little exercise and whose health is said to have been fragile.[25] On 23 April 1358 the French royal court attended a magnificent tournament and banquet to which all the knights of Europe were invited and given safe conduct, regardless of their allegiances. It was one of the few highlights of that year, however, since on 22 or 23 August the doughty Isabella, friend to the French captives, died after a short illness. She had her last dealings with the French court on 15 July.

Soon after her burial in the London Greyfriars in November, the English attitude to their royal captive and his court began to harden and by winter they had decided to move him, partly when the extent of Isabella's former personal part in wholly unofficial negotiations began to come to light, partly in response to French sabre rattling, itself a retort for the increasingly bitter struggle for that kingdom. English armies, kicking their heels during a period of truce, ranged unchecked and ill-disciplined as they foraged across her northern provinces and encountered an intense and brutal revolt of her own peasantry (the so-called 'Jacquerie') against the rather inept Dauphin, Charles, who ruled shakily in his father's name. Headless since Poitiers, France was now virtually lawless.

The spoils of Jean's capture continued to excite the exchequer and throughout 1358 and 1359 moneys changed hands for a whole variety of valuable goods which had once belonged to the French king. Much of it was taken and sold by the Black Prince, or was bought by him from others. They included the magnificent silver ship (a nef, probably a table centre signifying the ship of state), taken from the king's camp after the battle, the crown and the silver star (the eponymous chivalric badge) and his own Bible.[26] In a bitter irony which seemed to echo Jean's own country's fortune, the silver ship of state was broken up, half its value going to a group of Cheshire archers who laid claim to it as booty from Poitiers.

Evidence for the hardening attitude came with orders in December 1358 for Jean and his immediate court to move to Somerton Castle in Lincolnshire, a former residence of Isabella herself, but one which was probably cramped by comparison with the Savoy, once described by Stowe as 'the fairest manor in all England'. Somerton had been a prison for English nobles as recently as 1355 so its security credentials were known.[27] However, the move did not take place at that time. Far from being power politics which deferred the move, the truth was far more mundane. Although the place was ready and the provisions delivered, the castle was 'burgled' as it awaited its guests. The felons evidently broke into the unguarded wine cellar and helped themselves to as many of the vintages as they pleased, leaving the barrels all tapped and opened, spoiling the wine.[28] The French royal court without wine, and wine provided by the King of England at that, was unthinkable. It would have been a matter of embarrassment to Edward III had the move gone ahead. However, for the meantime the wind had changed and the remaining stay at the Savoy was under guard, although Jean continued to enjoy the regular hospitality of the members of the English nobility.

When Jean did move, it was not to Somerton yet, but rather to the familiar surroundings of the late Queen Isabella's former home at Hertford Castle on 4 April 1359. The move was helped by the provision of a convoy of eleven removal wagons from the French-born Countess of Warenne, such was the bulk of goods they had to take, including a church organ which had to be brought specially from London. Even then they forgot a portable altar which was inadvertently left behind at the Savoy and had to be specifically sent for in time for Easter. A flurry of activity before Easter attests the importance of having everything ready in time for this, the most important feast in the Christian calendar. Jean even had a special engraved 'wafer-iron' ordered for the Easter Communion (a sort of pastry-cutter flattener and fancy embosser to make the communion wafers). It caused a problem as the engraving made its delivery late.

Here at Hertford can best be seen the captive court at work and play. There survives remarkable evidence for this period in the form of French expense accounts and what amounts to shopping lists to keep them in the manner in which they were accustomed. They span the period 1 July 1359–8 July 1360 and thus cover much of Jean's captivity. Even the names of the servants are known from these detailed accounts.[29]

Hertford Castle was, and remains, a prominent landmark within the town. It is today a pretty shaded garden, fringed and well watered now, as then, by the River Lea (or Lee) and its tributary the Mimram. Of the castle itself, little remains above ground but the imposing feudal motte and the square inner bailey, ringed by a high flint wall which retains a fourteenth-century postern gate and a polygonal mural tower. A huge lawn marks the location of most of the castle buildings in which Jean and his court would have been lodged. Only 40 miles, or a long day's ride, from London, the site was ideal.

Under the overall direction of the king's chamberlain, Jean de Dainville, the court and its accounts were divided up into six areas of responsibility – the *Panneterie* (clothing, laundry, repairs), the *Eschanconnerie* (cellar), the *Cuisine* (kitchen), the *Fruiterie* (fruit, herbs, spices and medicines), the *Escurie* (stables) and the *Fourrière* (accommodation). Prince Philippe had his own small band of attendants and the workings of the royal chapel had its own staff, ten strong. Since there was a limit to the numbers of the court, some individuals served in a number of different roles, such as one of the chaplains who was also the prince's falconer while another was also the king's physician.

The *Panneterie* accounts involve a great deal of making-do and mending for most, except for the king and his immediate circle. Huge sums were spent on furs, mostly large numbers of minivers (European squirrel) from Finland and northern Sweden, imported via the Baltic monopoly of the Hanseatic League. They were provided for the most fashionable London-based French costumiers, who took fourteen days over one suit. Over 1,900 were needed for just one hooded cloak and 600 for a greatcoat. After his first winter in England, Jean may have become painfully aware of England's singular weather and climate.

The cellar too dealt in large quantities on a regular basis. The court had barely arrived at Hertford when 16 tuns of wine (1 tun = 1,145 litres) arrived in April, the same amount in May, while in June a gift arrived, principally from Languedoc, of 214 tuns of wine, although on arrival only 168 tuns were found to be palatable. At 252 gallons per tun, that still amounts to a considerable wine-lake, and not a little vinegar. Late in June, the king's furrier in London, Adam de Bury, was paid partly in wine for his supply of the miniver furs, to the tune of 300 tuns.

The kitchen had mainly English staple fare to deal with, and ironically English cheese was much prized in France, but although the main meats and cereals were provided by Edward III's government, John's own kitchen staff included a Breton, who may have added his own people's delicate palate to fish dishes, while Robin le Saussier ensured that the addition of the latest French fashion for cooking in sauces was well catered for. Curiously, for the French court (at least through modern eyes) a local Hertford pastry-cook was employed, Saul Granssart.

The *fruiterie* dealt with fruit, conserves, herbs and drugs so was involved not only in sourcing the most expensive culinary tastes, but also in ensuring the king and his court's pharmaceutical needs were catered for, from pills to poultices and even a plaster for a head injury to a jester.

The stables were served by a group of six grooms, including a Gascon who was later promoted to the king's chamber. Their work was second nature in any royal and noble household as they all needed a variety of horses, whatever their circumstances. They would also have dealt with those belonging to the many visitors the court received. Evidence suggests that they may have been a rougher group than those of the 'household' proper, since on 25 May the groom Beraut knifed Mahiet d'Andelys, the Norman laundry maid, for which he had to pay her 5s recompense.

Those serving the accommodation would be responsible for sourcing firewood, tinder and fuel for the kitchens, which by this period also included coal which was available at Coventry (the North Warwickshire coalfield), one source already used by the Black Prince.

The days at Hertford were spent in much hunting and hawking, not least enlivened by joint parties with the English royal family, including one in which Prince Philippe's own hawk failed to return. It was later found by Edward III's own falconer and returned to the prince, whose considerable interest in the sport led him to have three new pairs of hawking gauntlets made. The young prince's outdoor pursuits were encouraged and a dozen crossbow bolts were sent from London, specially adapted with *bourgeois* (blunt points). While these may have been specifically for target shooting, and a safety precaution for a young man who was a valuable heir to the king (hunting accidents were not uncommon), it was also perhaps a matter of not providing too many weapons to a court in captivity and under constant English armed guard. If the guards felt themselves under threat, they might have become 'trigger-happy' among their very valuable charges.

As it was, hunting did not always go well. Jean and the court attended Mass at the nearby church of St Leonard's, Bengeo, one of a number of visits to this small Norman two-cell chapel which remarkably survives today in very much its original form with the addition of only a timber bell-cote and a brick south porch. While there, his hunting hounds broke loose and killed a sow belonging to the local Squire Revell, who lived adjacent. The apologetic king was forced to pay 10s recompense, twice the value of the previous knifing incident. It was perhaps doubly embarrassing since it happened outside the court.

Bengeo today is easily accessible by main road. In the fourteenth century the best way to it from Hertford Castle was across the numerous braids of the River Lea. Seemingly for just this kind of regular local journey, or maybe for fishing purposes, the king bought a boat from nearby Ware. However, seemingly because it turned out to be too small for his needs (or because the Hertford interlude would be all too short), he later returned it to the vendor, paying him 5s for the inconvenience the short-lived transaction had caused.

The evenings included a great deal of tomfoolery. As well as keeping at court a permanent minstrel-cum-playwright, Jehan Bonneamours, the king was very fond of his jester, also called Jehan, on whom almost as much was spent for clothes as the royal persons. In quieter times the king regularly played chess and spent money on a new chessboard and chessmen. He also sat for portraits and commissioned paintings from his court painter, Girart d'Orleans, who during the captivity painted the only surviving life portrait of the king. In an age before instant messaging and photography, to send such a portrait back was continuing proof to France that he was alive and in rude health.

It is during this stay at Hertford, where he probably already had a number of acquaintances from his previous visits to Isabella, that Jean's religious life in England comes to the fore. He seems to have struck up a friendship with the Abbot of St Albans Benedictine Abbey when he visited. He was received by Abbot Thomas de la Mare (abbot 1349–96) with fitting ceremony and they became sufficiently close for the abbot to confide in the king that he was intending to resign his office of ten years. Jean gave him encouragement and offered his support when the abbot tendered his resignation to Edward III; however, it was only the Black Prince who prevented his leaving by pointing out he was too good for the abbey to lose, having already rendered exceptional service when it was in grave need. The bond Abbot Thomas felt for King Jean was sufficiently strong for Thomas to ask the king's intervention when three men from St Albans were taken prisoner in France. The Black Prince wrote too to Jean, but the French king replied to Thomas that his request alone was sufficient to solicit his help.[30] Evidently the bond of friendship was mutual.

The stay at Hertford was all too short as the problems at Somerton were soon put right and the wine cellar re-stocked, perhaps partly by moving stocks from Hertford. There is, however, suggestion that some plotting with English rebels may have been going on from Hertford. English suspicions were running high, not least perhaps because the energetic but generally distrusted Cardinal Talleyrand was a personal friend and sponsor of Abbot Thomas de la Mare, and the two had met again (whether in Jean's presence is not known) before Talleyrand had left England in September 1358.[31] Talleyrand was known for his probity but he could not divest himself of English reticence to trust him. This was a pity since he had very strong links with England and had held numerous church benefices here for many years.[32]

Such suspicions perhaps made a sudden move all the more necessary. Certainly there was a very urgent need to buy more saddles on 27 July. On

26/27 July Edward III appointed Sir William d'Eyncourt and four fellow knights to take Jean and his court to Somerton and attend upon him there. Edward III took the opportunity to fetter the French king in a way he had not previously done, by reducing the size of his court considerably, by as much as thirty-five, thereby ostensibly down to twenty. Negotiation seems to have ensured that this crept back up to about forty, but it must represent a considerable curtailment of the king's operation, a sort of court for the provinces. Other courts pertaining to prisoners of Poitiers had their retinues sent back to France en masse so the king was certainly not being singled out for harsh treatment. Renewed security around Jean was sufficiently tight for the 29 July move to Somerton to be covered by a forty-two-strong armed guard.[33] They moved slowly, stopping at Puckeridge for a quaint-sounding picnic lunch on the first day, then to Royston, Huntingdon, Stamford, Easton-by-Stamford, Grantham and arriving at Somerton on Sunday 4 August, a five-day journey. Along the way Jean made generous gifts to the religious orders, typical of his spiritual largesse. The four-month stay at Hertford had cost almost £4,000. He had just remained solvent, not least thanks to loans from London merchants and the sale of some of his French wine.

At Somerton it was not intended that the French king should be out of sight and out of mind, but as a place of captivity it was isolated and inhospitable in comparison with Hertford, and the quarters are likely to have been comparatively cramped after Hertford. Somerton Castle was basically a four-square-walled enclosure of a manor house with towers at each corner and a gatehouse. Accommodation was in interior, freestanding and lean-to buildings, the gatehouse (for the guard) and the towers. Although Jean could, and did, enjoy the spiritual and mercantile delights of nearby Lincoln, where he maintained separate quarters for his visits, he was no longer in a position to be visited by numerous English magnates. Even if he had been close enough to London, he now lacked the space to entertain as he would be expected to do. With Isabella dead and the Prince of Wales back in France campaigning north of Paris after the expiry of a two-year truce, Jean's most genteel allies at court were gone. It was a time of introspection and relative self-sufficiency which would last throughout the autumn, winter and spring, well into 1360.

While sizeable amounts needed to be spent feeding and clothing the court, mainly out of London, it is the extras which continue to mark out the expenses as being out of the ordinary.[34] Jean continued to receive many considerable gifts of money from his nobles in France for the upkeep of his court, and the king continued to sell wine and horses here in England to help generate some income. He was also paying for cockfights, which were no doubt the subject of considerable wagers. On occasions he also had to pay for entertainment for royal visitors. In Lincoln Jean bought books, mainly religious and some poetry, along with parchment, paper, ink and sealing wax, not least since the court in exile generated its own business. Jean had quickly had a muniment chest made for him in London for just this purpose of official filing when still at the Savoy. He still had some considerable royal duties to perform, even if they were in his absence from his kingdom. Among the books, Jean had an old French Bible re-covered and given new clasps, his own travelling Bible having been captured at Poitiers (now in the British Museum).

That the court was always able to indulge a sweet tooth would be an understatement. The king's spicer and confectioner, Thomassin Doucet, was clearly well provided for as the following extract indicates:

> 23 kg loaf sugar, 4 kg moist sugar, 1.8kg white honey, 15.9l honey, 1 quartern of aniseed, 900g Cinnamon, 1.4kg root ginger, 250g cut ginger [crystallised], ½ quartern of long pepper, 450g galingale, 450g cloves, 250g mace, 450g grain of paradise, 5.45kg pine kernels, 1.8kg madriain, 450g nutmeg.

Spices were expensive since many had travelled a long way from the Far East to get to the spice markets of England, chiefly via the Venetian 'Flanders galleys' which annually docked in London and caused a public sensation when they landed their wares. Even to the royal court, the value of some of the spices can be gauged by the fact that Jean spent a considerable sum on a spice-box from a London goldsmith. A wide-ranging culinary expertise in the king's kitchen may be considered normal in relation to it. However, the above amounts may be misleading as, in order to provide for the court and its guests, the volumes on this particular shopping list may have been ahead of a special entertainment. Even though they might be kept in the best conditions possible for the day, some would have spoiled if they had not been used relatively quickly. These were regular purchases and many large towns did hold regular, in some cases weekly, spice markets.

The young Prince Philippe appears to have taken up a considerable expense. Besides his love of hunting and hawking, not in itself of note but perhaps interesting in contrast to his father the king, whose tastes were more literary and cerebral. Expenses for Philippe alone betoken a princely penchant for sports and shoes, dozens of pairs of them, bought at London, together with clothing of the finest materials. This is the tell-tale upbringing of the youth who would later become a *bon-viveur*, the art-loving and ostentatious Philip the Bold, Duke of Burgundy.

If outdoor pursuits occupied Prince Philippe, they could not detract from just how isolated Somerton must have felt for a royal court used to France's grandest castles. Little survives of Somerton Castle today, just a single tower jutting awkwardly out of a later house and its modern working farm, but the considerable quadrilateral earthworks around it show what a well-proportioned circuit it once had. Its drawback is its topography, an emptiness of almost treeless, flat land all around. It is a place of endless fields and wind-marshalled clouds where a hundred ravens can be heard to laugh manically when the wind drops. Today, hardly a soul passes by. In the imagination it is truly a place of exile.

As if to note this time in exile and how slowly it might pass, Jean also bought a clock. This was not as sad as it might seem since, once out of the sight and sounds of London or Lincoln or (now a distant memory) St Albans, few church bells tolled the hour and every court in the land had to move and work to the rhythms of the day and the available hours of daylight. Although attended by his own chaplain as confessor, for his devotions Jean also attended Mass in the parish church at nearby Boothby Graffoe on a low ridge overlooking the castle some two kilometres distant on the road to Lincoln and Grantham. It was very much the same regimen he had been able to follow at Hertford, where he combined his trips out with visits to St Leonard's, Bengeo for Mass. Wherever he was, he gave generously to the churches.

Jean's one vice seems to have been his love of jewellery and during this time he had a number of newly bought gems, principally diamonds and rubies, put onto ring settings for him. One in particular drew comment, being a fine signet put onto a pendant. It comprised a yellow diamond in a crescent setting and surrounded by stars.

There was a downside to looking after the French court. Sir William d'Eyncourt may have been surrounded by the epitome of chic but his own purse did not allow him to easily partake of the full-time lifestyle into which he had been thrust, not least regular shopping trips into Lincoln. In fact there is evidence that Jean also took lodgings in Lincoln during the winter of 1359, perhaps because Somerton was proving to be inhospitable and so that he could observe Christmas in a fitting manner at Lincoln Cathedral. Sir William's plight became so difficult in December 1359 that he received financial help from the Crown in the form of a total tax rebate on all his manors across the East Midlands as he had been unable to attend to any of his affairs, being utterly preoccupied in the full-time task of keeping King Jean fed, entertained and guarded.[35]

For both prisoner and jailer alike, however, a change of air was not long in coming. With the end of the winter, rumours began circulating of a French plot to spring Jean from his prison, made all the more real by French raids in force on the port of Winchelsea (Sussex). Thus at the beginning of March 1360 Edward began to make arrangements for Jean to be brought back to the Tower of London, but not directly. First of all he was to go to the castle of Berkhamsted in Hertfordshire while the necessary re-shuffling of rooms and suites took place at the Tower. This took about three weeks to arrange since

Berkhamsted was a manor that belonged not to the king but to Edward the Black Prince.[36]

Berkhamsted might never have been considered as an ideal place of residence for King Jean since it is known not to have been in very good condition. Only a short while before, the great tower had been 'split in two places' and needed a new roof. Many of its principal buildings and rooms were in need of repair and attention.[37] It was, however, a castle with a recent reputation. Only the previous year, 1359, the coroner had held an inquest into the death of a prisoner there while in custody. However, the whole area was known to be suffering and some fields had still not been sown with crops since the Black Death of 1349.[38] Such suffering was not lost on the French king, whose own plight stood in stark contrast to the people's lingering difficulties. His ransom negotiations, still dragging on, might help to alleviate this social malaise in both England (through payment) and France (by his return home).

Berkhamsted Castle today remains a sturdy, grassed earthwork with considerable lengths of flint curtain walling surviving. Its motte is very high and improbably steep. The earthworks of the ramparts are today the location for a curtain of tall trees which tend to obscure the castle from the outside and lend an air of seclusion from the town's bustle once inside. In the fourteenth century, with no such treeline, the view would have been across the natural bowl in which the castle sits, out to the ridge of hills which cradle both castle and town on three sides.

The stay at Berkhamsted lasted a few weeks only. Certainly by 27 April the king was once more in London, this time at the Tower, where he seems to have been assigned new quarters. These may not have been quite as commodious as before since his own expenses include having to construct new casement windows for his own chamber. He also began to entertain once more and was able to make forays out under guard, including rowing on the Thames to Rotherhithe where many nobles had fine town houses. He amused himself at the king's menagerie at the Tower, even contributing to the upkeep of Edward III's lions there. Surely this must have been a huge, if bitterly ironic, joke on everyone's part; as the King of England was hobbled by his war with France, the King of France was in the Tower and the doubly captive king of beasts was being fed by them both.

Although negotiations over his own ransom were proceeding well, if still painfully slowly, the relative helplessness of his own plight was still not lost on him and, perhaps out of a sense of solidarity and compassion, he made generous gifts of money to the inmates of Newgate Prison. For some this may even have been enough to buy their freedom. It is highly likely that among them were countrymen of his own.

Agreement was reached on his ransom and Jean's own freedom finally came on 19 May 1360, after only a few weeks back in the Tower. The constraints on his travel were removed and he enjoyed the same privileges which had been granted him in the early days at the Savoy. In June he was entertained at Dover, where he climbed the heights above the town with the English royal family. He was once more entertained in the town in July when everyone exchanged parting gifts in a show of brotherly affection. He then crossed to Calais where he stayed a while before moving into France proper when arrangements could be made for his return to government and the reoccupation of his palaces with his court. In the months to come Edward continued to shower his former prisoner with gifts, particularly sumptuous jewellery, especially rings of the highest quality, set with the finest precious stones.[39] Not everyone was happy with his release and, as if to warn of dire consequences and imply heaven's disquiet with a wholly bad decision, Thomas Walsingham juxtaposed the news of his release on earth with dreadful heavenly portents and hearsay that the devil incarnate walked the earth.[40] Presumably he spoke with a French accent.

Part of the bargain for Jean's release was the exchange for a long list of hostages who would come to England and submit themselves to temporary exile while the French king raised the balance of his ransom, the down payment having been made. The list of hostages was notable, in so far as their pedigree as royal lieutenants was impeccable, effectively ensuring that any anti-English resistance could not coalesce under the returning Jean. They comprised Prince Louis (Duke of Anjou and Jean's middle son), the Duke of Orleans (with Louis making recompense for his apparent cowardice at Poitiers), and the dukes of Bourbon and Berri. To these were added the counts of Longueville (who could not avoid it this time after his previous let-off after Poitiers), Blois, Alençon, St Pol, Harcourt, Portien, Valentin, Beaumont, Brême, Foreste, de Couci, de Preaux, Valentin, St Venant, Garentières, Hangeste, Montmorency, Danseurs and Auvergne, along with William de Craonne, Louis de Harcourt, Jean Hugayne and other lesser dignitaries whom even the contemporary chroniclers omit to name.[41]

In early 1362 and 1363 two hostages, the Counts of the Auvergne and St Venant, petitioned the Pope to be allowed home, one on account of age and failing health, another to attend to business matters.[42] It is presumed their requests were formally passed on to the English Crown and granted. Another, Count Enguerrand de Couci, previously instrumental in 1359 in putting down the 'Jacquerie' revolt in France, became much attached to England, marrying into English local nobility, and was granted lands in Lancashire. Meanwhile, although free and actively trying to raise the money for his ransom, as well as finding time to marry for a second time (to Jeanne of Auvergne in 1360), Jean himself had not forgotten the many friends he had made in England and in 1363 was petitioning for the foundation of a nunnery on behalf of one new friend the Duke of Clarence at Bruisard, Norfolk.[43]

Both before and after Jean's release, negotiations had also been progressing on the release of the many other individual nobles who had been captured with their king. Prince Philippe was returned with King Jean, but separate deals had been struck on the likes of the counts of Sancerre and Craonne and the Archbishop of Le Mans, captured by the Earl of Warwick.[44] They had been quartered all over England for up to four years. Not all his fellow captives were as lucky. The Lord d'Aubigny remained in captivity as a hostage, and in 1361 was transferred to the forbidding Tickhill Castle (Yorkshire).

Meanwhile King Jean back in France had been having meetings with the King of Cyprus who was raising money and support for a crusade on a journey that had already taken him across most of Northern Europe. Having deliberated for some time, at Easter 1363 and before the Pope in Avignon and the College of Cardinals, Jean took the cross and placed himself under a vow of crusade along with some of his most trusted knights. The King of Cyprus was said to be exultant with the decision. Jean was now under the Church's protection, along with his dominions.[45]

It would all end in tears, however. On 6 December 1363, Prince Louis, Duke of Anjou, together with a small group of companions, broke his parole and made it to France. The now crusading King Jean, hugely inconvenienced by his son's actions, was mortified and, anxious to preserve his chivalric reputation, jeopardised by his own son, returned to England with a small court. Under vow of crusade he could do nothing other. Once more he was lodged in the appropriate surroundings of the Savoy. Impressed by the honourable nature of the man he always called his 'Adversary of France', Edward III and Queen Philippa sumptuously entertained Jean at Eltham Palace at some point over the Christmas period 1363 and waited excitedly at the gates for his arrival. There were dances and (presumably French) carols sung for his benefit and the young anglophile hostage, Count Enguerrand de Couci, distinguished himself by singing and dancing in his king's honour. Jean was asked to join in but in reply let slip his displeasure at his lot by echoing the biblical psalm remembering Israel's own exile. He answered, 'How can I sing [the Lord's song] in a strange land?'[46]

He remained no stranger to entertainment, however, and within a short time he was dined by the former Mayor of London and well-known vintner, Henry Picard, whose dinner-guests on one single night comprised at top table Edward III, Jean II of France, David II of Scotland and the King of Cyprus, together with Edward the Black Prince. Without doubt the King of Cyprus was pointedly continuing his Europe-wide recruiting drive to the coming crusade, and at the very least angling to see his highest-profile recruit released at the first opportunity. The opportunity to canvass the support of three kings and the Black Prince was too much to pass up. After supper Picard maintained open house (so all could see his largesse and his connections) and challenged all comers to games of dice and chance. He had good reason to be such an amiable and effusive host since, even disregarding that he had the finest of wines in his cellar, he had arranged loans for King Jean in 1359, and in 1363/34 he was the official royal receiver of the king's ransom.[47] In view of this, it is highly likely that France paid the bar bill that night, whether they realised it or not.

With the fading Christmas festivities went hopes of a simple solution. With £47,000 already in the bank, but with much more to come, negotiations received the ultimate shock when in April 1364 Jean died suddenly after a short illness.[48] It was an embarrassment to everyone although no blame was laid at anyone's door since, with the possible exception of a period of relative isolation at Somerton, he had enjoyed the best of everything and had been treated like the king he was, and now in addition a crusader. Edward ensured that a trusted knight, Sir Nicholas d'Amoury, was sent with guards to act as a suitable cortège and accompanied King Jean's body to Canterbury and Dover and handed it over to his countrymen. The following day he made arrangements for an obituary Mass to be said in St Paul's to mark Jean's passing and timed to coincide with his burial at St Denis in Paris.[49]

The business of redeeming prisoners and hostages continued behind the scenes for some fourteen years in all and the reckoning for Poitiers was not over until 1370/71, in which year ransoms were still being paid and hostages were still being freed from all over England.[50] Poitiers had been a battle that emasculated the French aristocracy and drained their coffers for a generation. The royal captivity that followed it defined Jean II's reign forever.

3

'ALAS I AM ALONE!'

CHARLES, DUKE OF ORLEANS, IN ENGLAND (1415–40)

As many as 1,500 prisoners were taken at the Battle of Agincourt. However, none was more valuable than the twenty-year-old Charles, Duke of Orleans, pulled out bloodied but miraculously unharmed from under a heap of twisted corpses, some of the more than 6,000 French dead. Along with him were the Duke of Bourbon, and the counts of Eu, Vendôme and Richemont, together with Boucicault, Marshall of France, and the lords of Humières, Roye and Connoy, Ligne and Noyelle, Inchy and Ancob, along with numerous of the foremost knights of France.[1]

They were treated courteously and taken quickly to Calais, to be joined along the way by prisoners taken previously at the fall of Harfleur and elsewhere. The principal prisoners were provided with an off-the-peg suit of clothes, which was probably an affront to their best French sense of fashion, as keen in the fifteenth century as it remains today, but it probably felt better than travelling long distances in what remained of their soiled and dented plate armour and hot, padded jerkins!

An exceptionally poor Channel crossing in appalling weather lasted a full five days, but on reaching Dover the prisoners and their guard made for London via Canterbury, Rochester and Eltham. At the capital a civic delegation met them and they were fêted in the streets, very much as Jean II had been more than half a century before. The next day, Charles turned twenty-one.

Soon after Charles's arrival in England, Henry V issued his shopping list for the duke and his fellow prisoners' comforts in their initial prisons, comprising the Tower, Eltham Palace, Westminster and Windsor Castle. It makes remarkable reading:

Lace curtains, 'travers', lint (felt), fustians, counterpanes, blankets, 'coopertor', bolts of worsted cloth, woven tapestries, pallet beds, canvas, featherbeds, materials 'and other diverse necessary things', linen from

Champagne, Flanders, Brabant and Westphalia, bolster pillows and satin.[2]

The Duke of Orleans seems to have been one of the prisoners who enjoyed Windsor Castle, Berkshire, at this time, a time for setting up new courts and preparing for a long stay. He had not been away from home too long and Charles spent a great deal of time busying himself in prayer for his deliverance and arranging gifts for his second wife, Bonne, and his young daughter Jeanne back in France. He arranged for a jester to continue to entertain them in his absence. He was initially given over to the care of William Loveneye, along with the Duke of Bourbon and others, Windsor being big enough to accommodate many of them at once.[3]

In the same month of December 1415 the king issued safe conduct passes for the five falconers of John,[4] Duke of Bourbon, to return to France, presumably for his stock of birds (and no doubt to pass vital information in both directions), while the Duke of Orleans's personal servants, Hugh Perrier and Ralf Nantel, received their permission to join their master, crossing at the same time with his personal valet who acted as his messenger. After Agincourt many of the noble French prisoners would have arrived in England with very little but the clothes on their backs, and the royal purchases on their behalf would have been most welcome and a measure of their victor's magnanimity. At this time the Duke of Bourbon was delivered of 100 tuns of wine from the king.

Not everything he needed could be provided by the English and early in 1416 Charles sent home for additional clothes and bedclothes.[5] His closest servants, Hugh Perrier and Ralph Nantel, came and went almost freely, although not without official sanction.

By spring 1416 the full mechanism of the Church's negotiating power swung into action and there arrived Sigismund, King of the Romans, the Count of Hainault and the Archbishop of Rheims. Henry V was even forced to give up the Palace of Westminster to accommodate their retinues. However, their efforts came to nothing as the French prisoners were divided in their attitudes, the Duke of Bourbon trying to negotiate for himself at the expense of his fellow countrymen. By the end of August all the negotiators had gone, their various alliances with Henry actually stronger.

At the beginning of 1417 Charles was sufficiently happy with his lot to agree to vouch for the safety of English ambassadors going to France to seek peace,[6] although at the same time Henry raised a fleet and invaded Normandy once more, perhaps an early follower of the adage 'speak softly but carry a big stick'!

Mildly cosseted, Charles's own shopping lists paid dividends and in March 1417 his servants turned up with a long list of goods, including six pairs of green hose and twelve headdresses. Most of his clothing was stamped with his arms, in an age when outward show was very important and his own existing unmarked livery would have been unfamiliar among the numerous badges and liveries of the English court. Along with clothing they brought the ducal wardrobe, such as enamelled ivory-handled razors and brushes and evidence of a sweet tooth – 3 lbs of nougat from Lombardy and 7 lbs of quince marmalade.[7]

On 1 June 1417 Henry issued orders for Charles to be moved from Windsor. He was moved by Sir Robert Waterton to Pontefract Castle, Yorkshire, where he would join others from his former circle.[8] Clearly he had amassed a court too large for his jailer to manage since horses had to be commandeered for the move. Bourbon soon followed out of Windsor, but he went to Portchester, near Portsmouth, for a while before being moved via Somerton Castle in Lincolnshire, probably kept separate because he had tried to negotiate for his own release and not that of the others and in doing so had distanced himself.[9] He was moved eventually under Sir Robert Waterton to Pontefract by the end of October where they were all provided with huge quantities of wine from Henry V.[10] It is at about this time that Pontefract Castle gained a new, enlarged bakehouse and brewhouse, doubtless to accommodate its new noble prisoners and the large numbers in their courts.

Others of the prisoners taken in France did not get moved quite so freely. For the first two years after their capture a group of seventeen largely unnamed knights, many from Harfleur, were held in the Tower of London, in the charge of James, King of Scotland, while the other foremost prisoners of Agincourt were kept at Fotheringhay Castle in Northamptonshire, where they racked up considerable expenses for their jailer, Sir Thomas Burton.[11]

While the Yorkshire air might have agreed with Charles, the association with Pontefract was darker. Charles's first wife (and mother of his daughter, Jeanne) had been Isabella, formerly Queen of England and the hapless widow of the deposed Richard II whose death there in suspicious circumstances in 1399 must have left Charles in no doubt that his first wife's stories of her own first husband's grim death held a grain of truth.

Charles was, however, given a degree of freedom and was able to visit Waterton's home in nearby Methley, 6 miles away, where he gave the family gifts. This closer association seems to have given the impression of unnecessary fraternisation. Waterton may have fallen under the dashing young duke's spell and word reached the royal court, since on 1 October 1419, a suspicious Henry V, writing from campaign at Gisors, Normandy, rang the changes to keep even Waterton under scrutiny. Here we see a local answer to the age-old question 'Who guards the guards?'

To Thomas, Bishop of Durham and Chancellor of England:
Worshipful father in God, Right trusty and well-beloved, we greet you well!

The escape of the said Duke of Orleans, might never have been so harmful nor prejudicial to us, as it might be now … God forbid!

Therefore we trust you will see that Robert Waterton, for no trust, fair speech, nor promises that might be made to him, nor for any other reason be so blinded by the said duke, that he become more careless of his keeping; but see that he eschews all perils that may befall, and pay good attention to the secure keeping of his person as is possible.

And make enquiry if Robert Waterton uses any reckless governance about the keeping of the said duke and write to him and put him right.[12]

Pontefract was too far north and Waterton could not be trusted. The Duke of Orleans, and indeed Bourbon too, might be off and away before word could reach the king. It was too risky and the result was to have Charles moved again. Later that month, after little more than a year in Pontefract, Charles was moved south to join his captive countrymen at Fotheringhay, where the castle and village must have resembled a French outpost, just because of the numbers there. Deep in the most pleasant Northamptonshire countryside, surrounded by the most excellent hunting lands, the Duke of York had been buried in Fotheringhay's magnificent parish church, one of the few English nobles to be killed at Agincourt. Here they were all in the keeping of Sir Thomas Burton, who ran a tight ship, with the result that no French visits are recorded during 1419. This may also have been because English gains in Normandy were considerable at the time and the situation in France was foremost for the government. In 1419 even Château Gaillard fell to Henry, after a sixteen-month siege.

The 1420s brought great changes on both sides of the Channel. The Count of Richemont was freed and went to his brother the Duke of Brittany to try to solicit Breton support for England. In June 1420 the Duke of Bourbon was also allowed to return to France to meet Henry V on campaign and then to seek the funds to pay his own ransom, although he was only allowed to proceed under a heavy armed guard, which numbered fifty-nine under three trusted knights.[13] Charles's circle was beginning to dwindle. The stay at Fotheringhay was otherwise relatively uneventful and Charles was probably excited over the summer of 1420 by being allowed to visit London in June, perhaps to accompany the Duke of Bourbon part of the way, if only under guard.

The year 1421 brought the best and the worst of news from home. A setback came at Easter when his chamberlain, Charles le Bouteiller, was killed at the Battle of Baugey against the English. This removed the one man whose running of his duchy back in France was beyond reproach, and would make his own dealings with home more difficult. Home meanwhile brought the fine news of the marriage of his daughter Jeanne to the Duke of Alençon, strengthening personal ties in France.[14] Soon after, Henry V and his young royal French wife Queen Catherine made an official visit to France with their new young son, who would become Henry VI. Monstrelet notes that with the careful diplomacy and slightly patronising posturing that went on, it became clear that Henry had the measure of France and King Charles of France effectively became his vassal.[15]

Without returning to England, however, Henry fell ill with dysentery and although he lingered for some time, he died on 31 August 1422. Charles of France died soon after. Among Henry's last specific wishes to the regent, the Duke of Bedford, clearly written down in his will, was that the Duke of Orleans, the Count of Eu and others should not be released at least until Henry VI came of age, a further potential fifteen to eighteen years. Whether this development, effectively a major sentence of imprisonment, was communicated to Charles or not is not known but within a few months the new regime ensured he was moved again and in December 1422 he left Fotheringhay after four years. He may have hoped to have been reunited with the Count of Eu and others, who still remained in the custody of Robert Waterton.

However, it was not to be and he began perhaps the most isolated period of his captivity when Fotheringhay gave way to Bolingbroke Castle, Lincolnshire, a wild and isolated place after the lush and cosseted Fotheringhay. Here he was the ward of Sir John Comberworth who ran a very tight ship indeed and kept Charles in virtual solitary confinement (at least kept him out of the way of extra-mural interest). He did have the opportunity to go to Bourne and to Peterborough Abbey, while building work took place at Bolingbroke, and visited London during the summer of 1424. Later, at the end of that same year, during the winter of 1424/5 he was taken by Comberworth for an extended stay in London.[16]

There was perhaps only one redeeming feature about the stay first at Fotheringhay and then Bolingbroke, and that was the nearness of Charles to his younger brother Jean of Angoulême who was himself a prisoner of the English. From 1421, he was kept at Maxey Castle, near Peterborough, in less than acceptable conditions. While not actually mistreated, he was denied a healthy diet, and Charles's trips to Peterborough may have been partly linked to this situation. They were certainly in communication. Charles took every opportunity to seek sources of income for Jean so that he was better able to look after his own interests, securing the Orleans salt tax to help pay his way. This was brought to a head in 1424 since from Easter in that year it was decreed that all prisoners were to pay their own way in England, regardless of rank. Clearly Orleans and Bourbon (who had returned meanwhile) were becoming a serious drain on resources. That the Duke of Bedford as regent was also antagonistic may have played a part.[17] This, however, did not stop the jailers continuing to claim their own expenses year after year.

An increasing sense of isolation and impending poverty at Bolingbroke may have led to Charles selling a large amount of his furniture, furnishings, jewels and part of his library back at Blois. This may not have been too much of a personal loss as he had a library of almost a hundred volumes with him in England, to which he added constantly, on a variety of serious subjects, including medicine, in which he took a keen interest. However, his helplessness and solitude at Bolingbroke were compounded by the news in 1424 that his son-in-law Jean, Duke of Alençon, had been taken prisoner by the English at Verneuil. Both his beloved wife, Bonne, and his daughter Jeanne, were now without their husbands. By 1424 he had not seen Bonne for nine years, and as he turned in his solitude to writing soulful poetry, many ballads were addressed overtly to her. He remained desperately in love with her, and his ongoing pain at their separation was palpable.

As the war in France ebbed and flowed and France rallied initially behind Jeanne d'Arc, the maid of Orleans cited at her trial the hapless plight of Charles as the main motivation for her actions. She stated that God had revealed more about his situation than any other magnate. This would presumably have been the result of only divine intervention or some well-smuggled intelligence that had escaped Comberworth's notice since Bolingbroke continued to be a near-watertight prison of supreme isolation. One of his poems at this time laments, 'Alas, I am alone!'

The Bolingbroke years and their frustration stretched to seven years. Charles's near solitude meant that while provisions continued to arrive, they did so in not quite so prodigious quantities as before, such as 60 pipes of wine from May to June 1426.[18] Such alcohol would have seen his small court through the summer months when untainted drinking water supplies were not so trustworthy. In early November 1429, however, the situation changed when Henry VI was considered to have come of age and the influence of the Duke of Bedford began to be eclipsed. Charles was now seen with less alarm and suspicion, potentially less of a threat. Just after Christmas 1429, Charles was moved once more, this time to Ampthill Castle in Bedfordshire, built by a relative 'new man' and one of Charles's own creditors since 1412, Sir John Cornwall. Within a month Charles was allowed to visit London. His new situation must have been a breath of fresh air, but that there remained not even a whiff of his release.

Throughout 1430 a series of safe conduct passes were issued as Charles's new, laxer regime allowed retainers to come and go more freely and bring supplies, bought with his own money. Cornwall too was out of pocket and in May the king issued a warrant for the exchequer to pay his expenses on account of the duke, but added also the backdated expenses of his previous jailer, Sir John Comberworth, who still held the Duke of Bourbon. Both seem to have run up considerable debts, if their receipts are to be believed. Cornwall continued to claim well into 1432, to the tune of 400 marks.[19]

The year 1432 was one of deep despair and of frustrated hopes. It began with the devastating news of the death of the thirty-seven-year-old Charles's daughter Jeanne, aged just twenty-two and of whom Charles's memories were of a little girl of five. If this were not enough, soon after, his second and beloved wife, Bonne, died. She was still only in her thirties, but they had been parted for seventeen long years. Charles was disconsolate and his poetry, now reckoned to be a masterpiece of medieval French verse, became that of a man in despair, clearly very depressed. With this in mind it was perhaps a diplomatic masterstroke to move him once more, this time to a jailer whose own bereavement ran deep at the hands of the French. The new destination in August was at Wingfield Castle in Suffolk, the home of William de la Pole, Earl of Suffolk. William, only two years younger than Charles, was very much against the war with France, possibly not least because his father had been killed at Harfleur and his brother at Agincourt. Ironically only four years before, he had led the English besieging army at the very gates of Orleans itself.[20] He had also spent a short time in French captivity thereafter. Clearly both had reasons to be resentful of the other, but both shared a love of the arts, and in particular poetry. William's principal courts at both Wingfield and Ewelme in Oxfordshire had become known as places of artistic expression and civilised company.[21] Charles probably felt he was almost free and his poetry once more began to reflect this renewed hope.

With a new sense of purpose and the scent of freedom it was hoped Charles might become the core of a peace embassy to France. However, despite a stay of six weeks in 1434 under French noses at Dover in the company of the Duke of Bourbon, both still under guard, sufficient common ground could not be found to make the venture work. Charles, doubtless no longer in full grasp of the changing political scene in France, began to make concessions to Henry VI that amounted to up to a third of his homeland, which did not endear him to his countrymen. If his political grasp was slipping, so too was his mother tongue, after nineteen years' captivity. He is known by now to have been a fluent English speaker, something no doubt which helped win the attentions of a young woman at the Earl of Suffolk's court. He fell deeply in love with a woman believed to have been Anne Molins, cousin to the Countess of Suffolk, and marriage may even have been suggested, although their relationship did not quite eclipse the memory of his beloved Bonne.[22] Sadly it may have been this very thing which gave rise to Charles being moved once more, in May 1436, to Sterborough Castle, near Lingfield in

Surrey. For the moment he was destined to be unlucky in love. Alternatively, it may also have been a result of the nadir in trading relations that England was experiencing with France and her allies, England's entire wool export market collapsing briefly. Charles's diplomatic value closer to London may have been useful and in any case the Earl of Suffolk was recalled to military service, perhaps himself made all the more useful by the general intelligence he would have gained from four years in the close company of the Duke of Orleans.

Charles's new host, Sir Reginald Cobham, continued to be paid the accustomed 13s 4d per day, and money matters were now to the fore as the king seems to have decided on a ransom figure of £20,000 for Charles, who embarked on a frantic round of letter writing to get friends and relatives in France to raise the money.[23] The Duke of Brittany promised half alone. What might not be given might be raised by other means and in 1437 Charles sent jewellery to Bruges to be sold. In November of that year, he met his brother Jean of Angoulême once more, probably only their second meeting (at most) since they were parted when Jean was only twelve.[24]

In 1438, with Charles complaining in a poem that he was no longer adept at conversing in his mother tongue, he was drawing measurably closer to resolution to his long captivity. It was not helped by another move in July, this time to Stourton Castle in Wiltshire, as the guest of Sir John Stourton, who now joined a long list of jailers to claim expenses for their guest at the usual daily rate of 13s 4d.[25] While Henry VI had seemingly resolved on complete release, in order that the duke could help with peace negotiations between England and France, Charles had gained a valuable ally in the Duke of Burgundy who was actively campaigning on his behalf. A ransom remained necessary, however, but by December numerous guarantors had come forward, almost silencing those few individuals who still cautioned against his release. News of the impending end to his captivity was leaked and in January 1439, Pope Eugenius IV wrote to Henry VI praising him for the news, expressing his disappointment that good intentions had so far come to nothing.[26] It was perhaps not before time as Charles was complaining that his funding sources were rapidly drying up such that he was unable to pay his own bills. England set the ransom at 240,000 Ecus within six months and dependent upon the conclusion of a successful peace treaty with France. A down payment of 80,000 Ecus was stipulated. Unfortunately this took all of 1439 and well into 1440 to raise.

Early in the new year, Charles's custody was entrusted to the last of his jailers, Sir John Fanhope, who also joined the merry-go-round of expense claims, although this cannot have been as easy as previously since his prisoner was now moving around as the diplomatic pace quickened somewhat.[27] On 28 October 1440 Charles swore an oath at Westminster Abbey to keep his side of the diplomatic bargain, paid 80,000 Ecus upfront and was rewarded with his freedom. Sir John Fanhope was discharged from further duty as his guardian, as were the 100 troops who guarded him. Fanhope, perhaps out of a sense of chivalry, continued to accompany the duke on his return to France.

On 11 November Charles repeated his oath to the French at Gravelines before moving onto St Omer, where he married Mary of Cleves in the abbey church of St Bertin, a purely political union arranged by the Duke of Burgundy, Philip the Good, to whose recent representations Charles owed much.[28] Sir John Fanhope was his guest of honour and he is said to have paid him great honour and attention before he returned, his responsibilities discharged.

At the suggestion of Burgundy, the freed and newly married Duke of Orleans moved onto Bruges where he was fêted so royally he must have almost forgotten the privations of his captivity. He had been a prisoner for twenty-five years, captured barely out of his teens. He had had to stand helpless while his daughter grew up, married and died, while his wife grew towards middle age and herself died before the age of forty, and had whiled away his manhood, unfulfilled in love, in a foreign land where he even almost forgot how to speak his mother tongue.

Ironically, Charles may have been a victim not just of national power politics, but of personal greed. The medieval French historian Enguerrand de Monstrelet notes that sources close to the English court felt that the duke may have been released sooner had not his jailers received such generous expenses from the Crown. Since Orleans was required to find her own from at least 1424, at any point thereafter her change of heart and a refusal to have done so might have elicited Charles's release as his jailers' government income would have had to be spent. As it was they continued to coin it in, apparently without fear of having to pay anything.[29] Although this reasoning conveniently sidesteps the national issues, as if Anglo-French diplomacy were immaterial, if Monstrelet's sources were correct, how many of Charles's twenty-five years of captivity might have been spared had everyone acted honourably? It was a bitter and long-drawn-out codicil to the English victory at Agincourt all those years before.

4

THE COMPANY OF FRIENDS
EDWARD IV IN BRUGES (1470–71)

On 3 July 1468, Margaret of York married Charles the Bold, the Duke of Burgundy. It was a well-chosen union and the two would in the coming years become mutually supportive patrons of the arts in a partnership which brought only benefit to the Duchy of Burgundy, not least to its westerly outpost, Bruges, chief city of Flanders and the most magnificent trading centre in Western Europe.

Margaret was Charles's third wife and they married only eight days after they first met, but after two years of protracted diplomatic negotiations. The ceremony took place in the monastic Church of Our Lady in the city of Damme, 7 kilometres from Bruges. Lacking almost any kind of dowry (England was broke), their union warranted a low-key wedding breakfast in an unprepossessing house off the town square and only a stone's throw from the (presumably) rather noisome fish market where some 28 million Swedish herring were landed by barge during the fifteenth century. The town is today a gem of peace and quiet, ringed by the earthwork remains of its ramparts and filled with bookshops. The ruined church still stands, as does the house in which they celebrated their union. Their statues look down from the gothic town hall.

The newly-weds processed in majesty by canal into Bruges on a fabulous ducal barge to receive the acclamation of the city. The sumptuous festivities – feasting, dancing and celebration by day and night – which followed lasted a week and were the talk of all Europe.

The bride, Margaret, was sister to the beleaguered King Edward IV of England, whose kingdom was wracked by the Wars of the Roses and whose coffers ran so dry his sister's dowry could not be found beyond a down payment. Much was to be provided by Italian merchants who were largely neither pro-English nor pro-Burgundian, but pro-trade, as both states were vital to their interests. Margaret's marriage was an alliance that bound

England and Burgundy against a sabre-rattling France while for Edward it began a diplomatic courtship of his own that would be his salvation in his darkest hour. To seal the bond, the Duke of Burgundy also conferred on Edward the Order of the Golden Fleece, a singular honour, the nearest chivalric equivalent of which would be the English Order of the Garter.

The marriage would remain childless but Margaret did become stepmother and tutor to Charles's daughter, Mary of Burgundy, with whom she grew very close. She quickly became known as an astute and diplomatic duchess with a fine eye for the arts and keenly theological in her outlook.

The marriage almost did not take place. Agents of France and her allies, particularly Venice and Milan, sought their own alliance with England and tried at every turn to stop the union, announcing that they still thought it could be averted only weeks before the wedding.[1] They were probably at the root of scurrilous rumours about Margaret's previous love life and even suggestions of a love child. The incensed duke put the rumour-mongers in their place with a threat to have them thrown in Bruges's canals (which often doubled as the town sewers). This put the diplomats and agents of Venice and Milan in their place and they lined up alongside the other dignitaries and merchants to welcome the happy couple to Bruges on that July afternoon.

Alliances settled, Edward returned to England and a country increasingly at the mercy of the ambitious and manipulative Earl of Warwick. Edward, beloved by the common man, was becoming hard-pressed by the nobility who, at Warwick's stirring in the name of the former, deposed King Henry VI, were increasingly out of control. Information about the opposition from spies was relayed to Edward by his new brother-in-law who seemed to be better informed even than Edward. Indeed it was said of the duke that his 'recreation was businesse and ... delight extent of dominion' and he 'labor'd to disperse the storme before it fell upon England'.[2] The duke was incredulous that Edward seemed to take no notice. This is possibly because the duke also maintained close contacts with the Earl of Warwick and Edward could not yet be sure of his full support, or indeed the veracity of the intelligence. Regular dispatches got through from foreign spies about the chaos into which England was spiralling and the strengthening of existing alliances, as opposing powers each tried to thwart the other:

Sforza de Bettini to the Duke of Milan
Tours, 20 November 1469
From England no two reports are the same, but differ like day from night ... King Edward has a large army which has deserted Warwick ... The king has received the Order of the Golden Fleece from the Duke of Burgundy as an additional sign of their alliance.[3]

The next year brought only more misery for England, with neither side sufficiently in the ascendant to win convincingly, although hostilities increased. Rumour and reality mingled as late 1468 saw a plot against Edward brutally quashed and early 1469 a raid in force by English armed merchantmen into Aquitaine (guaranteed to keep French hackles raised). Intelligence in early December 1469 suggested that Edward would be reinforced by levies from the Duke of Burgundy, further aggravating France. A treaty with Spain left France between a rock and a hard place. There was much posturing and manoeuvring and much of the diplomatic traffic of Western Europe was paralysed by the lack of a decisive outcome as the English parties seemed to waver equally between uneasy truce and open hostility, each trying to make Burgundy and France show their respective hand in a dangerous game of brinkmanship.

Sforza de Bettini to the Duke of Milan
Tours, 8 December 1469
No other news from England, save that the king is still said to be very well established, and the war between the king and Earl of Warwick is greater than ever. M de Concressault [messenger of France] still waits in Normandy without going further till the result of affairs in England are known.[4]

Tours, 13 March 1470
Nothing else from England, except that the king and the Earl of Warwick are well agreed together, though as yet it is not known that they are arming to attack France, although it is suspected.[5]

Meanwhile Warwick went to France to secure a treaty against Edward, who was increasingly disadvantaged by the turn of events. By the middle of June 1470, news indicated that the Duke of Burgundy was raising a fleet to go to Edward's aid, a move welcomed by Edward no doubt, but one which might be used by his detractors to paint him as a despot propped up by an interfering foreign power. In a last-ditch effort this fleet blockaded the English coast to prevent Warwick returning, since an England–France alliance was not in Edward's or Burgundy's interests. They failed and he slipped through with a fresh army to cause havoc in the South. Meanwhile the North rebelled and Edward was forced to take notice; but he was too late. Squeezed between North and South, he was taken into custody probably either at Olney (Bucks) or near the fiercely Lancastrian city of Coventry where the Earl of Warwick camped with 30,000 troops.[6] One historian relates that Edward was lodged nearby, where the Archbishop of York seems to have forced himself into his bedchamber, and was briefly taken under house arrest to nearby Warwick

Castle.[7] Politically emasculated by the Earl of Warwick, Edward's plight was becoming desperate and his support, although still there, was finding no opportunity to coalesce.

With nowhere to turn, Edward and his closest supporters took to their heels during a lull, chased first north-east through Nottinghamshire and Lincolnshire, before making for King's Lynn. This left the diplomatic community awash with rumour and poor intelligence, summed up in a letter from the partisan Bishop of Navarra:

> Bishop Giovanni Archimboldo to the Duke of Milan:
> Mont Richard, 12 October 1470
> King Edward is a fugitive and in hiding, his whereabouts being unknown, for which reason the Duke of Burgundy has broken into an ill temper and is much alarmed.[8]

The Milanese ambassador to the French court wrote home to his master the Duke of Milan that Edward 'fled in disguise aboard a fishing boat'.[9] His own (undisguised) glee at Edward's flight found voice in his debasing of the details. The king was not in disguise and the boat was fully chartered. However, the ambassador's understanding of the diplomatic situation was correct in asserting his destination, the country of the Duke of Burgundy. He was now a political exile seeking foreign support for his very existence.

Despite Lancastrian sympathies, a contemporary chronicler (John Warkworth) was matter-of-fact about the dire straits in which the fleeing king found himself:

> Kynge Edwarde haysted hym in alle that he miyght to the towne of Lynne, and ther he toke schyppynge one Michaelmesse day, in the X yere of his regne ... overe the see into Flanders, to his brother in lawe the Duke of Burgeyne, for socoure and helpe.[10]

In reality the contemporary language did little to point up what unseemly haste it actually was. Edward embarked with nothing but the clothes on his back, even having to leave behind the royal treasure. Few of the 800 or so friends, relatives, retainers and soldiers who followed quickly in his wake had any more to their name. Edward was (apparently) forced by his penury to pay the master of his ship with the gift of his own cloak. This may have been a genuine gift but in a medieval world of inner meaning it was a gesture which was reminiscent of St Martin, a saint whose gift of his cloak led directly to his road to salvation. St Martin has always enjoyed a special place in the religious lore of West Flanders and news of the gift would not have been lost on his intended hosts. Although it is largely lost on a modern English audience, William Habington, writing in 1640, at a time of great religious intensity, also noted that the gown was lined with the fur of pine martens, if further allusion were needed.[11]

The little fleet, headed by Edward and his brother the Duke of Gloucester (later Richard III) and his brother-in-law Charles, Lord Scales of Worcester and William Lord Hastings, was joined at sea by a number of vessels from the Netherlands. They were harried all the way across by vessels belonging to towns of the Hanseatic League, whose economic well-being was being affected by England's unrest. They were forced to put in briefly at Alkmaar, near Haarlem, but were escorted out once more by a small armed flotilla sent by Louis de Gruuthuse, a man who had been a friend of Edward, ambassador to England and a fellow Knight of the Golden Fleece. On 7 October 1470 they made landfall at The Hague. Just off their stern lay ships serving the Earl of Warwick in pursuit, but the Duke of Burgundy put his ports on alert to deter any hostile landing a few days later. Edward stayed at The Hague for a fortnight before setting out to meet his brother-in-law, Charles, Duke of Burgundy, informally. He spent Christmas at Ardenbourg before coming on 27 December to Gruuthuse Castle at Oostcamp, near Bruges.[12] After a brief journey to Aire-en-Artois where he met with the dowager duchess of the Burgundian court, Isabelle of Portugal, he returned to Gruuthuse Castle at Oostcamp, via St Pol, where on 9 January he wrote to Francis II, Duke of Brittany to solicit his support. On 13 January Louis de Gruuthuse offered Edward and his court the hospitality of his palace in the fabulously defended city of Bruges, which Edward gratefully accepted.

This magnificent manor was nothing short of the kind of palatial apartments Edward was used to. Arranged around a central court, and standing close by the principal parish church of Bruges, the Gruuthuse Palace is today a museum but externally is little changed from the buildings Edward knew. Edward had apparently wanted to occupy the same house on the Market Square that he had enjoyed during his sister's wedding celebrations in 1468, but the political situation meant he could not be sufficiently guarded there as he would have needed a round-the-clock watch.[13] The self-contained Gruuthuse Palace instead was perfectly defensible against spies and would-be assassins and it also enjoyed one of the most focal locations in the medieval city, with Edward at the heart of civic affairs, something Oostcamp could not have afforded him.

Edward's court was no mean act to support. Although shorn of its wealth, its members were used to relative luxury, a heady combination of expectation and cost! The nobility alone was notable: Edward; Richard, Duke of Gloucester; Charles, Lord Scales of Worcester; Lord Hastings; Lord Bath, the Duke and Lady Exeter; Lady Suffolk; Lady Cecille; Lady Holland; the Countess of Suffolk; Earl Rivers; Lord Sele; Lord Montagu and the Earl of Oxford, called in Brussels 'the most virtuous and dignified knight'. These were billeted around the city in the homes of wealthy individuals who were well disposed to the cultured English court, which had given them their beloved duchess. Most notable was Charles, Lord Worcester, who was put up by Josse de Bul on Sint Jacobstraet at the Hospital of St Josse, next to the Baudets Gate and the stoutly defended town ramparts.

Without means, the court was reliant on the hospitality of friends and the city of Bruges was unstinting as host. Perhaps mindful of the prodigious consumption during the wedding festivities of 1468, the magistrate of the nearby town of Furnes sent 6 pipes of wine for the thirsty court. The city itself put up £25 immediately for the generous Louis to defray his own initial outlay. More money was promised from the duke shortly, while the English merchants in Bruges all chipped in.

As guests of honour Edward and his court were immediately pitched into the religious and courtly round of Bruges's civic life. The king took part in religious festivals and processions, that of the Holy Blood on 6 February out to the convent of St Claire and again ten days later when the phial of Christ's supposedly still-liquid blood was carried out through the Marshall's Gate to the (now destroyed) Hospital of St Madeleine. Known for his command of both Latin and French, he was able to take advantage of the extensive library of Louis de Gruuthuse, known as one of the most extensive of its day, and it is here that Edward, with a little time on his hands, may have written a play, a comedy entitled *The Whore of Babylon*.[14] The court was also immersed in the flourishing artistic output of the city, dominated at the time by Bruges's new darling of the art world, Hans Memling. Edward maintained his religious duties and his piety took a new turn as he is said to have formed a particular devotion to St Anne during his exile.[15] St Anne was known for her literacy (in particular, legend has her teaching her daughter, the Virgin Mary, to read and write). Given this devotion Edward almost certainly worshipped at the triple-aisled medieval church of St Anne in Bruges, subsequently re-designed in the baroque style.

Medieval Bruges existed for the purpose of trade and Edward's presence was quickly to become both a blessing and a curse to this. The king soon met England's man in Bruges, William Caxton, loyal Yorkist and for twenty-five years head of the English trading 'House', the permanent legation whose former headquarters remains one of the most sumptuous buildings in the city, now an extensive 'Georgian' pile. Caxton had courted the arts of his adopted home and his experiences went some way to facilitating his efforts to begin printing in England.

To this day Bruges remains magnificent. Fortunately the canals are no longer the sewers but also sadly are no longer the bustling highways they once were. Neatly revetted in stone and largely cleared for the fleets of tourist taxis that power back and forth, the former banks are gone. Once they were home to voles and water rats and 10,000 piles supported wharves and jetties everywhere, at which 1,000 boats were tethered (anchors puncture the clay canal lining), bobbing gently in a light swell when the wind blew, setting rigging rat-tatting against creaking masts, every so often a crane straining between them to unload a cargo. Here each year through the medieval period the wealth of the Mediterranean was unloaded, brought up the canal from Damme and Sluis and the Zwin estuary beyond, landed from the magnificent Flanders galleys sent from Venice, loaded with everything exotic. Their merchants vied with those of every other major state in Europe to land the best cargoes and get the best prices. English woollen cloth, Indian spices, miniver (squirrel fur) from Finland, iron from Spain, salt from Brittany and wine from Bordeaux, Atlantic cod and Swedish herring by the thousand, to name but a few. A considerable portion of Western Europe's international trade was moved through here.

Ensconced in the sumptuous Gruuthuse Palace, externally still little changed from the 1470s, Edward might have been considered well out of harm's way. Here he was able to indulge his passion for the arts and literature, taking advantage of Louis de Gruuthuse's magnificent personal art collection (including the work of Memling) and library, which was the rival of any royal collection. However, his ongoing presence was a problem for others. Bruges's hunger for England's woollen cloth (whether under Edward or Warwick) was considerable, and the open alliance which Charles the Bold was forced to maintain with Edward quickly began to unsettle others, whose trade was either with England under Warwick's influence or with France. The latter forced Charles's hand when in December she declared war on Burgundy who now badly needed an English ally with some power behind her. What she quickly deduced that she had was a landless exile whose chance of regaining power receded daily. Where once Edward's power guaranteed Burgundy's trading position and acted as a balance to France, his presence as exile now threatened to undermine it.

Edward's view of Charles, meanwhile, was also altering. Although he was still the dutiful host as his brother-in-law, the openness of Charles's unbroken dealings with the Earl of Warwick caused Edward's demeanour to cool and 'he never bore the duke so much sincere affection as before'.[16] It was not helped by the stream of displeasing intelligence from England. The queen, already heavily pregnant when the flight from King's Lynn took place, was shut up in Westminster Abbey in her own internal exile, and here she gave birth to a son, an heir without a kingdom.[17]

Meanwhile the pitiful figure of a broken Henry VI, released from the Tower, was given a second Coronation at St Paul's. He was swathed in Edward's voluminous regal robes, which almost drowned his emaciated frame. There was no apparent residue of support for Edward and England seemingly now had a new king, Warwick's pathetic puppet. The state papers of the day explained the change by Edward having abrogated his responsibility, 'having made a journey to parts beyond the sea, ... no one being left in his place as lord or guardian of his kingdom ... and his justices did not come hither'.[18] Henry's so-called 're-adeption' of his kingdom was officially back dated to when Edward 'toke shyppynge', Michaelmas Day 1470. Parliament met and fell in behind the puppet Henry. Deadly proscriptions cut a swathe through the English nobility as Warwick's new regime in Henry's name sought to legitimise its hold on England. Edward was now king in name only and his whole future lay in others' hands. He must move quickly or watch helpless as Henry's re-formed government attempted to take a firm grip.

Just as Edward was becoming wary of his brother-in-law, so too did Charles's dealings with Edward now become acutely difficult. The duke's position was made most embarrassing by his growing awareness that in Edward he now harboured nothing more than a powerless, deposed ex-king, and was faced with an England whose alliance with a resurgent France now found voice in Henry. He was the newly crowned head of state and, however pathetic, was one with whom France could legitimately deal and co-ordinate her campaign against Burgundy. To add to his woes, Bruges's trade routes were under pressure, with the fabulous annual visit of the Venetian state galleys already being preyed upon by pirates in the Atlantic and the Channel. They were forced to form convoy with others for mutual protection from the Isle of Wight onward, the English fleets which normally protected them being conspicuous by their absence.[19]

The money which Charles had promised was now forthcoming, all at once, in a flood designed to give Edward the wherewithal to make his play for his kingdom – or die trying. Charles was not minded to mince his words and diplomacy went out of the window. The private gift of 100,000 Ridders was clearly marked 'for his and his brother the Duke of Gloucester's expenses ... and for their departure from my lord the duke's lands to return to England'.[20] Thus there was no further option of living out a cultured but perhaps restrained exile among friends, although the duchess, as a concerned sister, pressed Edward to be patient and stay longer for his own safety, perhaps a little naïvely, since as each day went by the re-formed government of Henry VI grew a little stronger and its alliance with France began to blossom. The duke, concerned that his trade with and through England was being choked off and his military position was becoming more desperate, lost all patience and, as Habington put it, was 'distempered with an ague of discourtesy' towards his brother-in-law on first a weekly but then a daily basis.[21] He made him wait until January for a full audience; his growing displeasure was plain.

Edward took the unveiled hint and, in concert with the duke's agents, made arrangements to hire ships and mercenaries and made plans to leave Bruges to reclaim his kingdom.

A date of 29 February was fixed for Edward to sail out; not before time as on 12 February English troops in Northern France were to join the French push into Flanders. Bruges was well able to defend itself and would continue to arm itself through the 1470s at the singular Louis de Gruuthuse's expense but a joint Anglo-French attack so soon was bad news.[22] Following Edward's attendance at the procession of the Holy Blood on 16 February, rumours circulated of his imminent departure. The next day he was contacted by a French delegation who, aware that all was not well and fishing for news, asked him how he would look back upon his time in Flanders when (or perhaps 'if') he regained his throne.[23] They were clearly seeking some assurance as to whether the Anglo–French treaty against Burgundy had a future under him. His answer is not recorded.

The *Warkworth Chronicle* reports 900 Englishmen and 300 Flemish hand gunners (*arquebusiers*), were kitted out for the king; together with a compact force of ships on which they were set to embark.[24] In all, picking up supporters along the way, the force would eventually number some 2,000.[25] Contemporary chroniclers who harboured Lancastrian sympathies, attempted to foment distrust of Edward, making out that the force was entirely foreign mercenaries (and by implication meddling in England's sovereign affairs) but the core was indeed English. They were to sail from Zeeland in a mixed fleet provided partly by Charles (four ships), Hanseatic merchantmen (four more) and a motley flotilla of others they had brought with them the previous autumn or could hire.

Being the consummate diplomat, Charles's privately disgruntled demeanour was not reflected in public, of course, and his preparations for Edward's send-off spared no expense. He fitted out three great ocean-going barges, opulently 'tiled' (probably rigid polychrome tile floors and walls below decks) to take the royal court from Bruges to Damme, Sluis and the Zwin and on to Veere on the Scheldt estuary, where they would embark aboard their fleet out of sight of prying eyes and the range of prattling tongues.

Leaving no one out of his public generosity, Charles gave gifts of personalised books to Edward's court, each decorated (presumably inlaid or embossed) with the white rose of York. As the fruits of William Caxton's twenty-five-year stay would soon demonstrate, Bruges's printing pedigree had become the focus of Northern European literature.

On 29 February, as Edward's barges made their way north to the speyer (water gate) towards Damme, the so-called Dampoort, they increasingly found their progress slowed by an unusual number of craft, not the usual daily press of barges ferrying goods from the estuary, but smaller, private skiffs and dinghies, joining them from left and right, oars clanking in their rowlocks in a cacophonous drumbeat of expectation. Hundreds were turning out to see the tall, handsome king and wish him well.

They glided past the Carmelite Friary and St Anne's church; past the turning to the English merchants' house where even now William Caxton was packing his own bags to follow his Yorkist master, recalled with him to England after twenty-five years. The convoy of barges slid, bumped and scraped its way towards the city walls and the speyer, which gave access to the open canal to Damme, only 7 km beyond.

However, as they neared the water gate the throng of boats with their excited well-wishers became impassable and it became clear that all the duke's efforts to fit out the magnificent barges for his brother-in-law would come to nothing. At the city limits Edward was forced to put in to the bank and his entire party was forced to disembark, where, at over 6 feet tall, he stood out in any crowd. He and his closest companions diverted to the house of a friend for refreshment (Jean de Gros) then took to walking along the canal bank. Here, with water on one side and the flat farmland of the polders (reclaimed land) on the other, their route could not easily be blocked and the crowds would have to follow on behind. Freed from the traffic jam of goodwill, the king's baggage would follow in the ensuing hours on the barges.

The majority of the journey to Damme today is very much as Edward would have known. Beyond the city suburbs the canal, neatly fringed by plane trees, slices though the polders, which are criss-crossed by drainage ditches and endless pollarded willows, thirstily drinking what the ditches cannot drain. Once dried out this land is fertile, and its soft going is excellent for training horses, the ditches and fences ideal for jump training. The canal has always been a haven for wildlife. Even today, less than a kilometre from the edge of modern Bruges, the traveller is met by scores of coots, tufted ducks and mallards, mingling with the herring gulls whose seaside home is only a few kilometres further north, and for which the Damme herring market would have provided a daily feast.

Naturally, the waterway from Bruges to Damme (and Sluis and the Zwin estuary beyond) would not have been flanked by cycle paths and a main road as it is today, but the ordinary path alongside the canal would finally have afforded Edward a pleasant walk, with his closest retainers, of about an hour and a half. They would not have dawdled on a chilly February morning, the leaves not yet on the trees.

Despite the coldness of the morning, and the increasing awkwardness of Edward's relationship with his brother-in-law, the king's send-off had been as genuinely warm as any could have wished for. The dispossessed English court in exile had caught the public imagination of Bruges, whose first glimpse of Edward had been at the sumptuous marriage celebrations of 1468. He was handsome, cultured and brave and they had taken him to their hearts. With this short walk began the journey back to England. It would be delayed by bad weather and embarkation only took place on 11 March from Flushing. Aboard the *Anthony*, Edward first made landfall at Cromer, Norfolk, but was repulsed. He soon after disembarked successfully at Ravenspur in Yorkshire.

The flustered Italian spies continued to follow events in their breathless correspondence. Sforza de Bettini wrote to the Duke of Milan from Beauvais on 9 April 1471 that Edward had landed with 5,000–6,000 troops (exaggerating) but had been routed with high casualties. He went on that the king had taken refuge in a church, adding, 'They think he will leave his skin there.'[26]

Their intelligence was wrong and out of date as Edward, moving south, picked up support and handled each new political challenge deftly. Lancastrian hopes were to be dashed when at the Battle of Barnet on 14 April the second reign of Edward IV of York began. He later wrote to the citizens of Bruges to thank them for their gracious hospitality, while the begrudging Venetians wrote to congratulate him on 'most justly' regaining his kingdom.[27] Trade resumed greater than before.

5

ROOMS WITH NO VIEW

HENRY VI IN THE TOWER (1471) & HENRY TUDOR (HENRY VII) IN BRITTANY (1471–85)

The pathetic figure of Henry VI, whose re-adeption of the throne of England in 1470/71 was so brief, was on Edward IVs return a shadow of his former self.

During his long and eventful first reign (1422–61) his court had been cultured but riven by strife and rivalries which went unchecked. Ominously, at Henry's last, year-long parliament, in Coventry in 1460/1, the crown was said to have fallen from his head onto the floor.[1] At the Battle of Northampton in 1461, his party came to bloody grief and Edward IV had ascended the throne while Henry was taken prisoner. However, he escaped his captors and fled to Scotland with his wife, Queen Margaret, the daughter of the Duke of Anjou, whose Franco-Scottish links were relatively strong.

While Edward reigned, Henry's position out of sight made him powerless. However, he made a brief foray into England, but met with no success at the Battle of Hexham (May 1464), although he was not actually there in person, being in the nearby castle at Bywell. He fled, leaving his regalia behind and abandoning his Northern supporters, who were largely imprisoned or executed. His already frail physical and psychological state gave way and he descended into a state of delusion and mental detachment, supported by few, other than his immediate family.

Not long after, he slipped into England in disguise, a ruse which was thought at the time to be complete madness for a king whose appearance ought to reflect his rank. He spent the next few months travelling around Lancashire and the Lake District, where he still retained a few supporters. He was entertained at Crackenthorpe, near Appleby, on numerous occasions, and spent time in the high Furness Fells, between Coniston Water and Lake Windermere, wild country beyond Edward's easy reach. He then made his way south and west along the Ribble Valley and stayed at Bolton-by-Bowland and at nearby Sawley Abbey. By the end of June 1465 he was staying at

Waddington Hall, near Clitheroe. There on 29 June he was given away by a Benedictine monk while sat down to dinner. A scuffle ensued as his hosts tried to protect him and usher him out. After a sunset chase of a few miles back towards Clitheroe he was overhauled, probably now in near darkness, as he gingerly crossed the 'Bungerley Hyppingstones', stepping stones over the Ribble in a nearby wood called Clitherwood.[2]

Polydore Vergil is more prosaic, saying simply that he was 'taken by the watche', but that probably simply alludes to a guard placed at the crossing of the Ribble.[3] From there he went to the Tower. There he was attended by two squires, a chaplain, two yeomen of the Crown and their men. Far from being immediately vilified, 'every manne was suffred to come and speke with him, by license of the kepers'.[4] This may have been because he was a broken man; to reassure any who might still waver in their support for Edward that Henry was clearly too fragile a character to rule the kingdom. Otherwise this almost open access to the former king seems inexplicable since he might hatch a plan for an escape (it was possible to break out of the Tower, and some did). Mental illness of one form or another might ensure a degree of care was afforded him, at least while the situation remained unchanged. His captors were rewarded handsomely for their prize and the expenses they incurred in capturing the former English court.[5] Henry remained in the Tower until his re-adeption under the watchful eye of the Earl of Warwick in late 1470, a move which sealed his fate.

When Edward IV returned from Bruges, his defeat of Henry and the Earl of Warwick at the Battle of Barnet in April 1471 brought a sudden halt to the Wars of the Roses. With Warwick and many of his adherents killed in battle, the Lancastrian sting had been drawn. Henry was returned to the Tower and it is the months of April and May 1471 which draw the most comment and, from much of history, the greatest condemnation.

Henry had been in the Tower almost continuously since 1465. It was not necessarily the place of horror with which later generations have imbued it. It was, after all, a royal palace and had been such since the days of William the Conqueror. State apartments there might be more or less comfortable depending upon the status and favour of the prisoner being confined. During his imprisonment, Henry remained known as Henry of Windsor and regular payments out of the exchequer (either side of his brief period of freedom) indicate that he was provided with the basic necessities of life and something else besides, as befitted his station, but without being gratuitous. Thus he was provided with a new wardrobe of clothes and new beds, suggesting that he was not moved into his old (1465–70) apartments but allotted new ones, in changed, perhaps stricter, times. From his arrival on or around 23 April 1471, he was assigned two squires, Robert Ratcliff and William Sayer, and up to thirty-six other attendants. Of these perhaps ten seem to have been in constant attendance from early May.[6] All were retained for the 'safe custody of Henry'.

After the Battle of Barnet, the country remained in a state of near insurrection and Lancastrian forces were still capable of coalescing. Although their principal war leaders had largely been killed, Henry still had influential supporters in the Western Midlands and the West Country. Accordingly when a scratch force of Lancastrians under the former Queen Margaret and young Edward, formerly Prince of Wales, met Edward IV's army at Tewkesbury on 4 May, they had high hopes of keeping the flame burning, at least on a regional basis. However, it was not to be and the hastily mustered Lancastrians were routed with great bloodshed. Among them fell the Prince of Wales, whose visible death in the ranks sent the watching Queen Margaret into a steep decline. She herself was captured and was initially well cared for in relative isolation.[7] The Lancastrian cause seemed doomed.

For the former King Henry VI, time was now very short indeed. His death in the Tower, days after Tewkesbury, brought cries of foul play almost immediately, but they were not universal, probably since he had enjoyed neither good physical nor mental health for so long. History, it seems, has always looked to apportion blame. The earliest record (almost contemporary), in the relatively balanced *Fleetwood Chronicle*, states,

> When news [of Tewkesbury] came to the sayd Henry, late called kyng, being in the Tower of London … he toke it so great despite ire and indignation, that, of pure displeasure, and melancholy, he dyed the 23rd day of the monthe of May.[8]

It would not be out of keeping with Henry's known mental and physical state. Suicide is also possible, although none would mention it, so appalling would that have been to the Church. Others soon sprang to cry foul play and point the finger of accusation. Lancastrian in tone (but not rabidly so), John Warkworth states,

> The same nyghte that Kyng Edwarde came to London, kynge Henry, beynge inwarde in presone in the Toure of Londone, was put to deathe, the 21st day of Maij, on a tywesday nyght, betwyx 11 and 12 of the cloke, beynge thenne at the Toure the Duke of Gloucester, brothere to Kynge Edwarde, and many other.[9]

There is a lack of evidence as to how Henry died, and those who reported it across Europe went with their political inclination. Word travelled fast, although fact mingled seamlessly with baseless rumour. The hand of Richard,

Duke of Gloucester, was quickly suspected, but that he might act without Edward's connivance seemed impossible.

Sforza de Bettini to the Duke of Milan
Feria, 17 June 1471
King Edward has not chosen any longer to have the custody of King Henry ... The prince his son and the Earl of Warwick have perished. All his most powerful adherents have shared the same fate or are in the Tower of London, where he himself is a prisoner. King Edward has had him put to death secretly, and is said to have done the like by the queen, the consort of King Henry. He has in short chosen to crush the seed.

It seems that on account of this cruelty the people of England made some demonstrations of a rising against King Edward, but there being neither head nor tail, the thing was soon suppressed, and thus King Edward remains pacific king and dominator of that realm of England, without having any longer the slightest obstacle.[10]

It is not the intention of this book to examine the forensic detail of if, how or why Henry was killed, but suffice to say that it would have been folly to surround him with so many witnesses (between ten and thirty-six), all charged with his safe keeping, if it was intended for him to be killed. The Tower was at the time also a hive of activity, specifically full of workmen and troops from Calais who were busy strengthening the fortress amid a general alarm. Conversely one advance payment made by the exchequer for Henry's diet was surprisingly small, suggesting that he may already have been considered ill and was not expected to overly trouble the accountants.[11]

Whatever rumour threw up in the days following Henry's death, no expense was spared on his funeral. Following the embalming of his body, which apparently continued to bleed from the nose as he lay in state,[12] a solemn procession wound from the Tower to St Paul's where the coffin was guarded by soldiers from Calais. One comment made at the time suggests that access to his body was severely restricted (feeding suspicion): 'abowte the beer mure glevys and stavys than torches' (around the bier more swords and cudgels than torches).[13] Then, wrapped in 28 yards of Dutch linen, his body was rowed by barge along the River Thames for burial at Chertsey Abbey, his rites accompanied by Masses sung by Carmelites, Augustinians, Franciscans and Dominicans.[14]

Thereafter a few desultory proscriptions were acted out, while others were imprisoned or banished, such as the Earl of Oxford, who was imprisoned at Hammes Castle, near Calais. A twenty-year truce was concluded with Scotland, to prevent it becoming a haven for former Lancastrians (and thus allow for extradition proceedings where appropriate). On 11 May 1471, days after the Battle of Tewkesbury, Queen Margaret was brought to King Edward at Coventry, before being taken to London, where she was held for the next four years. It is unclear whether between Margaret's appearance before Edward (11 May) and Henry's death (23 May) any opportunity occurred for them to meet. If she was sent to London soon after the 11 May audience at Coventry, there may well have been a few precious days when she was in custody in London, tantalisingly close, before his death.

In 1475, after prolonged negotiations, Margaret was ransomed by the French king, Louis XI, and allowed to go to her kinsmen in Anjou. In the issue rolls is the payment of the escort which accompanied Margaret 'lately called the queen' to Sandwich on her way into final exile.[15] There she 'lyvyd in perpetuall moorning', although her lot grew steadily more poverty-stricken as her status was bargained away and her remaining claims, both English and Angevin, dwindled to nothing. [16]

Only one heir to the House of Lancaster yet remained more or less untouched by Edward's runaway successes at Barnet and Tewkesbury. Across in south-east Wales the fifteen-year-old Henry Tudor had already lived most of his childhood as a hostage at the imposing honey-coloured Raglan Castle, ward of the cultured and Welsh-speaking Herbert family, where in 1471, he was 'kept as prysoner, but honourably browght up'.[17] However, he was about to grow up quickly as Edward had realised that here was a young and vital figurehead around whom his enemies might rally; he is said to have described him as 'thonely ympe now left of Henry VIth's bloode ... he adjudgyd this onely thing to disturb all his felycytie'.[18] Freed since the re-adeption of Henry VI, the success of Edward had turned the tables once more and the young Henry's uncle and mentor, Jasper Tudor (half-brother to the dead King Henry), now decided to take the youngster out of harm's way as surviving Lancastrians fled the bloody field of Tewkesbury. Edward's concern was clearly not without foundation as it was recorded by Sforza de Bettini, the Milanese spy, that Louis XI, instigated by the Duke of Milan, sought to foment disturbances in Wales under the leadership of Jasper Tudor, who was being directly financed through the French king, although it was acknowledged that the chances of his success might be slim.[19]

The two fugitives seem to have been back at Raglan briefly, perhaps to say some goodbyes, since Henry and Jasper were almost captured at Chepstow where they had to cross the River Wye. Soon, however, they were indeed captured at Pembroke Castle where they had been recognised. Friends aided their escape once more and they made for Tenby where they were forced to hide in a cellar on the High Street. On 2 June 1471, less than a month after Tewkesbury, the two, with a few friends and retainers, hastily boarded a ship, 'a barke peparyd out of hand',[20] for France and the court of

Louis XI, friendly in as much as it was distanced from Edward by his recent exile in Bruges.

The long, looping course, which a route from the Pembrokeshire coast requires, around Cornwall and into the Atlantic led them into difficult Channel currents and winds and the treacherous north coast of Brittany. The ship ran ever westward before an unfavourable wind and they made landfall not in France but at Brest (Finisterre), at the western tip of Brittany, a Duchy which maintained an uneasy truce with England through its duke, Francis II, whose help Edward had sought during his own exile in Bruges. Its relationship with France was equally uneasy and this made for a safe haven for the moment. In any case the young Henry was Earl of Richmond in waiting, and this seat had very long association with the independent dukes of Brittany, going all the way back to Pierre Mauclerc in 1218 who first held both titles together.

From Brest the two Lancastrian nobles would have sought an audience with the duke, which may have taken some time and would probably have been held far to the east at Nantes, the fabulous capital of the duchy, at his sumptuous new castle and palace, begun in 1466 and still under construction. They cannot fail to have been moved by the cultural and artistic cutting edge that the ducal court at Nantes wielded amid astonishing surroundings. The duke was said to have 'receavyd them willingly' and took the trouble to address them at length, making great play of the 'young princeling's' escape from danger and taking him by the hand amid much laughter to break the ice.[21] The French historian Commynes also noted how gracious the duke was, and that he gave them permission to move freely within his duchy, although this promise was never really to lead to any real freedoms. They could certainly not return home, where domestic matters were further muddled when Henry's mother was widowed from his stepfather and remarried to a confirmed, prominent Yorkist within the year. Edward, at first gently, began a campaign to get 'thonely ympe' returned to England by diplomatic means.

Where the two were originally put up is not altogether clear – Nantes seems likely; some freedom of movement may be inferred for a while. However, by 1474, with Henry now eighteen and of age, Edward IV's attentions grew more alarmist 'Pembroke having been upon all occasions an open rebel, and Richmond onely wanting age to take armes, and who shortly appeared to threaten no lesse dangerous'.[22] Richard, Duke of Gloucester, advised the king to send an embassy to Brittany to seek Henry's release to England's 'care'. Duke Francis, knowing that it would mean he would be releasing Henry into extreme danger, answered that it would do his own reputation all the more good not to do this, while keeping the hostages out of harm's way meant Edward was under no obvious threat.[23] He even paid Edward's embassy off.[24]

This, however, marked a turning point in Henry's fortunes. Now of age and clearly seen as a threat to the status quo and at the same time as a bargaining chip, Duke Francis openly moved and separated the hostages, making it known to Edward that he was doing so. Jasper Tudor was sent to the magnificent, many turreted Rohan family fortress on the River Oust at Josselin (Morbihan), then undergoing huge structural changes.

The young Henry, however, was sent to an infernal place 20 miles north-east of Vannes (Morbihan) at the castle of Largoët, deep in the Elven Forest, sometimes called Elven Towers. Surrounded by deep woodland, even today it is an astoundingly isolated place, encircled by a 60-foot-wide moat (now dry) fed from an infernal and possibly malarial lake wherein fish break the still, stygian-black surface. At one side of the castle stands in cold grey stone what is today the tallest keep in France (57 m), property of the Rieux family, Marshalls of Brittany.

Here, on the first floor, next to his guards, is the ogee-vaulted prison bedroom of Henry Tudor, future King of England. It measures 10 feet by 7 feet, space enough merely for a bed, and lit only by a narrow 10-inch-wide slit at the end of a gash in the 10-foot-thick wall. It is the ultimate *room with no view* as it looks out alongside the keep portcullis mechanism into the inner courtyard.

Isolation was Duke Francis's idea, intending that the hostages 'should be in a free but a safe custody, in a countrey where they were so farre from power, that they wanted acquaintance. And that himselfe would narrowly looke that no discontented persons should resort to them, or that they should worke their addresses to any other prince.'[25]

As if this infernal place were not secluded enough, Duke Francis now took away both Henry's and Jasper's households, replacing them with Breton servants, whose own language was close enough to the hostage's native Welsh to facilitate communication but to prevent any secrecy. They were charged with observation rather than service, and their duty was to report the hostages' every word and look, to interpret them and to send word to England.[26] All communication of any kind between Henry and Jasper in their two prisons was banned. William Habington astutely observed with hindsight that it is possible that this period played psychologically into Henry's hands, because the effect was to make Henry think more highly of himself since Edward (through Francis) was paying him so much attention. However, so secluded was Largoët, as Habington observes 'whereas had he lived unsuspected by the king; he had perhaps dyed unobserved by the world'.[27]

After at least eighteen months of close confinement at Largoët, Henry was sent north in response to another embassy from England, headed by the Bishop of Bath and Wells. Edward gave assurances that he merely wanted to nullify the Lancastrian threat by marrying Henry into his own family. Few believed it, including Henry, who, 'knowynge that he was caryd to his death, through agony of mynde fell long the way into a fever'.[28] Advisors to Duke Francis remonstrated with him, noting pointedly, but deferently, that he had made the wrong decision, not least because a recent treaty between England and France appeared to make Henry, as Breton hostage, a rather more important bargaining chip. Accordingly Francis sent lieutenants after the embassy, which had reached the northern port of St Malo where the departure of the English embassy was delayed by adverse weather. Finding Henry they whisked him into sanctuary, being almost dead of his fever, according to both Polydore Vergil and William Habington.[29] The ambassadors took up arms to try to force him out but a local mob attacked them and defended Henry's religious right to safety in their church, anything else being sacrilegious.

His deliverance from the embassy was just the tonic he needed and Henry was 'delyveryd from feare of death, and by that occasion pretyly well amendyd'.[30] Imbued with a new sense of worth (in hostage terms), instead of being returned to his hellhole at Largoët, Henry was re-united with Jasper Tudor and they were now sent to far more commodious surroundings at the great port city of Vannes (Morbihan) on the gulf of Morbihan, where Henry would at least regain his strength and enjoy a cultured environment. They remained in separate custody, however. Jasper Tudor was in the care of Betrand du Parc while Henry was under the guard of Vincent de la Landelle. Although both probably spent time in the prison tower astride a gate in the city walls, both would have been quickly moved into private quarters, secure and under guard but on parole, given some degree of freedom around the magnificent walled city of Vannes, the so-called Old Town. They were allowed to travel out and regular visits were made to the sumptuous ducal hunting lodge of Suscinio Castle on the coast a few miles south-east of Vannes.

With a little more leeway, Henry was quickly able to begin a relationship with a local woman, her name now lost thanks to Henry's lifelong discretion; she bore him a son. The boy's early life is a closed book but he was named Roland de Vieilleville (of the Old Town) and in manhood was knighted and became constable of Beaumaris Castle on Anglesey. Born out of wedlock, Roland would never inherit and could lay no claim to the throne of England, despite being Henry's eldest son.

The hostages' lot was also improved by the Duke of Brittany's deteriorating mental health with the result that he simply took less notice of them. Duke Francis was said to have developed an 'extreame melancholly' bordering upon madness and rapidly became unfit for government.[31] Within a few years his death, as the last independent Duke of Brittany, would pave the way for the annexation of Brittany by France. For the moment, however, Henry and Jasper Tudor's new-found looser confinement allowed the laying of plans to return to England.

Back across the Channel in 1484, with Edward IV's reign having given way to that of his rather less scrupulous brother Richard III, the powerful Duke of Buckingham hatched a scheme to make Henry Tudor, now twenty-seven years old, king. Henry was loaned an army of 5,000 Bretons and a fleet of fifty ships to rise to the challenge. However, Buckingham's supporters in England deserted him and he was arrested, and not long after executed. Fortunately for Henry his invasion fleet was held out at sea by storms in the Channel and they were forced to retire, the news from England still unknown to them. Unable to put in, they were forced to regroup and return to Vannes, debriefing with Duke Francis at Rennes.[32]

The end of Henry's ordeal was not long in coming, however. The cruelties which marked the brief reign of Richard III only helped bring on a further attempt to re-establish the Lancastrian throne. With support through Wales almost guaranteed, the attempt this time was not to be a sailing-in force, nor one which involved the help of Duke Francis, whose continued diplomacy with England Henry feared was now probably one of self-interest alone.

Clandestine movement was now the plan and accordingly Henry slipped unnoticed out of Vannes with only five servants, one of whom was a guide, and taking the road east towards Anjou, where the count was 'family' although not overtly pro-Lancastrian. Henry was disguised as a servant to avoid alerting the city watch and a few miles outside the walls he and his party turned off into a wood for Henry to change his clothes. Meanwhile his 'small' court-in-exile of 300 remained in Vannes and went about their business as usual to avert suspicion that anything was amiss.

Henry and his small band rode hard for four days and nights without stopping, other than to water their horses, until they were in Anjou. When the ruse was discovered and Duke Francis heard what had transpired, he was enraged and expelled Henry's entire court from Vannes and his duchy. The court headed east for a reunion at Angers, the principal city of Anjou. Making swift preparations to invade England, Henry moved north, picking up support as he went. The Earl of Oxford, imprisoned at Hammes Castle (Calais) since at least 1474, came over to him, along with his guards and captors, turning Calais against Richard III. On 1 August 1485 Henry sailed from the mouth of the Seine with 2,000 troops.[33] Skirting the south coast of England, and entering the Bristol Channel, they arrived at Milford Haven in Wales seven days later. On 22 August Henry's forces, joined by allies old and new, defeated Richard III at Bosworth in Leicestershire in a battle which brought an end to the Wars of the Roses and ushered in a period of sorely needed national stability. Henry had spent almost all of his twenty-nine years as either a hostage or an exile. He now founded arguably England's strongest and most important royal dynasty as the two houses of York and Lancaster were united in that of the Tudors.

6

'EN MA FIN EST MON COMMENCEMENT'[1]

MARY, QUEEN OF SCOTS IN ENGLAND (1568–1587),[2] WITH A CONTRIBUTION BY SALLIE GEE

Many thousands of words have been written about this, described as 'one of the stormiest lives in British History'.[3] Little more can be written here to add materially to the controversy that has always surrounded, in particular, the death of this charismatic and controversial queen, whose designs on the English throne, thwarted in her own lifetime, were fully realised in the accession of her son (James I), her grandson (Charles I) and her descendants to this day.

Mary cannot be omitted from this book, however, because of two aspects of her life: her long and difficult captivity and her gender. As a woman she is almost unique because of the sheer volume of writing, both contemporary and subsequently, that she has occasioned. The almost complete dominance of men as leaders and heads of state across Europe in the medieval period makes any study of royal and noble lives a necessarily male-dominated exercise. While many women accompanied husbands into exile, and some women chose or were forced into joint or parallel imprisonment or house arrest with their husbands, or occasionally in their own right, such as Eleanor of Brittany, the trail of relevant documentation is that much more tenuous and fragmentary. Mary is an exception, standing apart for her gender, and perhaps provides an insight into aspects of the female condition.[4]

When, on 16 May 1568, the twenty-five-year-old Mary crossed into England across the Solway Firth, she did so a fugitive, beaten in battle and seeking support from her cousin, Elizabeth I, against a rebellious Scots nobility, many of whom did not want her back. Elizabeth spent much of the next two decades unsure what to do about Mary, who abdicated in favour of her son James.

She landed at Workington in Cumbria, where she spent the first of only two nights of her life in England in relative freedom. The second was at nearby Cockermouth. She wrote to Elizabeth to solicit her support soon after landing and within two days was under the 'protection' of the governor of Carlisle, Lord Scrope, to whose town she was quickly moved. Her court was twenty-six strong and six women waited on her. Carlisle was a pleasant enough introduction to England and in mid-June conditions were lax enough for twenty of her court to play football outside the castle, although under the guard of a further twenty-two guards (history does not record whether a four-team tournament was a possibility!).

Her immediate guardian was Sir Francis Knollys, Elizabeth I's councillor, known for his erudition and learning, who wrote from Carlisle that these early weeks were marked by shortages. Mary wrote to him during her first weeks to ask him to intercede on her behalf with the queen.[5] With Mary forced to flee in haste, he wrote that she was very short of clothing, despite the arrival of three coffers of goods.

The English court was very wary of its new charge, and William Cecil, Lord Burghley (at the time Secretary of State), summed it up when he wrote, 'No access of English Scottish or French be suffered to come to hir without knolledg and allowance of such as have charge of hir and that good hede be taken to the apprehension of any letters that shall be secretly sent thyther.'[6] The tone of the next two decades was set.

Anxious to move Mary from harm's way so close to the Scots border, she was moved in mid-July to Bolton Castle in Yorkshire, still in the custody of Lord Scrope. Her shortage was beginning to wane since she arrived with twenty-four carts, twenty carriage horses, and twenty-three saddle horses, and within days this was augmented by five further cartloads and four horse-loads of goods.[7]

Knollys recorded his admiration for Scrope's house at Bolton, writing, 'This house appeareth to be very strong, very fair and very stately, after the old manner of building, and it is the highest walled house that I have seen.' As to the old manner of building, it in fact dates no earlier than the late fourteenth century so was much newer than some of the places in which Mary would be held, but Knollys was right in his observation of its sheer, almost featureless exterior walls. It can look a forbidding place. Its apartments all look inwards into a cobbled courtyard.

Letters written at the time said that Mary was 'merry and hunteth and passeth time daily in pleasant manner' so it cannot have been too onerous for her at this stage. Knollys also taught her to write in English while she was here, a skill which, if not learned very thoroughly, might be her undoing. Thirty-six retainers and six ladies-in-waiting were given permission to stay at the castle, while others had to find lodgings in the nearby village. Every day they came to the castle to be fed and warmed at Mary's expense. There were rumours of an escape attempt and in September Mary professed her Catholic faith openly in the Great Hall, causing great consternation down south, beginning a discussion about moving her to an area where she would find less sympathy.

Mary spent the first autumn and the best part of her first winter at Bolton, and almost immediately began to complain of the cold, sending for additional rugs and carpets to keep her feet warm. The court's consumption of wood became prodigious and fresh timber had to be felled as they outstripped the castle's supplies. Fodder too had become a serious matter by early November and the shortcomings of supplying the relatively isolated Bolton were becoming obvious.

Knollys soon began to tire of his charge at Bolton and wrote to ask for discharge. As the Catholic Duke of Norfolk came under suspicion for plotting against Elizabeth, his sister, Lady Scrope, also became an object of scrutiny and was quickly prevented from personal fraternisation. To prevent any coalescence of the Catholic faith around Mary, a more permanent and convenient lodging had to be found for her and it was decided that she should reside in the care and custody of the Earl and Countess of Shrewsbury. The earl was a relatively mild-mannered man, the fourth husband of the society firebrand, his countess, Bess of Hardwick. The ambitious and supremely focussed Bess has attracted many commentaries in her own right, some none too flattering. Traditionally she is said to have been 'proud, furious, selfish and unfeeling … she died … immensely rich and without a friend'. She was said to have 'sacrificed every principle of honour and affection [to riches]'.[8]

Knollys got his wish but the final days of preparation for Mary's move were fraught since Knollys's own wife died just as arrangements were being put in place. Ironically Mary's first letter in English had asked after Knollys's wife's health. Mary may have been expressing her compassion for him in his newly changed plight, as she protested that she would not go from Bolton willingly, knowing also perhaps that there she was still among sympathisers and her new abode was an unknown quantity.

Nevertheless the move went ahead. On 26 January 1569 the greatly increased royal 'train' began its journey to Tutbury Castle in Staffordshire, a place Mary would come to loathe. Thirty-six hired horses, borrowed from all over the North, including ten from the Bishop of Durham, women's side-saddles, six baggage wagons and eight carriage horses, all added to the long, snaking convoy which made its way to Ripon, Wetherby, Pontefract, Rotherham and thence to Tutbury. A short stop was made also near Chesterfield as Mary was said to be exhausted. Another, planned at Sheffield, was bypassed as the earl's manor there was being stripped to supply Tutbury, which they reached on 4 February.

Tutbury was by this date merely a hunting lodge for the earl and countess. It was cold, draughty and poorly provided for. So much had it been neglected that Mary herself observed that the plaster was coming off the walls with damp. On arrival she lamented that she had 'two little miserable rooms, so excessively cold, especially at night, that but for the ramparts and entrenchments of curtains and tapestry which I have had made, it would not be possible for me to stay in them in the daytime'. To add to her discomfort, these rooms had an exceptional view – over the castle vegetable garden. Beneath her window was the outfall of the castle garderobes (toilets) into cesspits with no drains. When they were emptied, she was assailed with the stench throughout her apartments.[9]

Although the Earl of Shrewsbury was to be allowed 6*d* per day for upkeep of forty people, there was an immediate cut in the numbers of her court. However this still included ten chief men, six valets, two men of the wardrobe, a tailor, a tapisser, two sumpters, three cooks, a paster and a baker. This was without her personal servants, their servants and the servants attached to the stables, fifty-nine in all.

It would be wrong to imagine that her new custodians were unfeeling towards Mary and her small army of retainers. They were well aware how unsuitable the castle was for lodging a person of note. The countess therefore took all the draught-beating wall hangings from her Sheffield manors for use there, while others were borrowed all the way from the Tower of London. While the queen may have only had two rooms purely to herself, the rest of her court was accommodated throughout the castle as a contemporary survey of the basic soft furnishings provided indicates:

Chamber hangings: Chambers hanged for herself only, the great chamber, her bed chamber and the chamber between for her grooms – 3; My lady Leviston's and Mistress Seaton's bedchamber – 2.

Bedding: Queen's bedchamber – 2 beds; Grooms' chamber – 2 beds; Lady Leviston's chamber – 2 beds for her and maids; Mistress Seaton's chamber – 2 beds for her and maid

She was still provided for as her station demanded, however, so the kitchen plate contained a great deal of silver, although in numbers just enough for her and her closest confidantes and advisers.

Mary's introduction to Tutbury was unusually gloomy as the spring of 1569 was locally very poor and she was forced to spend a lot of time indoors, which she chose to spend in needlework, a skill she enjoyed (and at which she was adept) and one on which she would spend many hundreds of hours through her captivity. For a while, her access to the countess was restricted, possibly after the suspicion that had surrounded Lady Scrope. There was no let-up in the new security and every morning soldiers searched beneath her window (possibly in the garderobe outfall) for any messages being smuggled out.[10]

The unfamiliarly poor conditions soon began to tell on Mary and she began to be affected by digestive problems. In late April she was transferred to South Wingfield Manor, not far away. Despite a quiet journey the change of air made little difference to her health and she acquired a bad stomach upset and was in considerable discomfort. This was swiftly used once more as a reason to move her and, still in great discomfort, she was taken to Chatsworth on a litter, the excuse being that her apartments needed proper cleaning. In actual fact this was probably nothing more than a smokescreen – a security measure, to search for incriminating evidence. On 1 June, after little more than six days, she was back at Wingfield where 240 people in all were staying. It seems to have been an unhealthy time since not only Mary languished for the summer; the Earl of Shrewsbury was also ill, such that he went to Buxton to take the waters, the Earl of Huntingdon briefly taking his place as Mary's custodian. The earl pressed for his charge to be moved to the more commodious Sheffield, but to no avail, and with her court down to thirty-two, and her spirits at a new low, she was moved back to the unpleasant Tutbury, which she already hated. On 25 September her personal coffers were searched.

Mary was unusually quiet at this time, not least because of security. A few letters did get out, including four to the French ambassador. It was suspected that she had written them in the dark. Assuming that no one had refused to provide her with candles, this was presumably suggested by some very poor handwriting. The Earl of Shrewsbury was carefully vetting inward correspondence, and kept messengers in temporary custody so as to stage-manage the process of reply.[11]

Mary remained ill for the rest of the summer and when the Northern Rebellion threatened to pitch her into the turmoil, she was quickly bundled south on 25 November to the walled city of Coventry. There the sources mainly disagree about where she stayed, mentioning the Bull Inn and the mayoress's chamber in St Mary's Hall, while the former Whitefriars Carmelite friary (then called Hales' Place) or some merchant's house had been sought but neither was forthcoming. With her court at over thirty people, it is likely that some were billeted in all these places. They were said to be all over the city, roaming unchecked. What is clear is that Mary was largely kept out of sight, so as not to stir up the populace, which had been courting the Catholic Queen Mary in the 1550s and was by reputation polarised. By 10 December Shrewsbury informed Elizabeth's court that the queen was lodged in a house, lately the Chief Baron's and the fittest in the city. This suggests abode at the Earl Marshall's house, which no longer stands, on Much Park Street. It would later house royalist officers when imprisoned in the city during the Civil War.

Mary remained in the city for Christmas, enduring some lewd preaching at her expense while she was there. She left on 2 January 1570, going back to the despised Tutbury. All was not gloom, however, and she was permitted periods of relative freedom; commentators called it 'fitful changes between leniency and rigour'. Mary was allowed out into the butts to practice her archery. Her aim may not have been too good, however, as she was showing the unpleasant symptoms of what seems to modern medicine to be conjunctivitis. During this year her court was saddened by the death at Chatsworth of John Beaton, the master of her household. He was buried at nearby Edensor, where his grave can still be seen.

Throughout the summer and autumn, Mary's health continued to give cause for concern and in November the earl and countess were given leave to move her to Sheffield, which provided better winter quarters. However, she continued to suffer terrible abdominal pain which now affected her sleep patterns throughout Christmas and into the New Year. Her physicians were her constant companions. Spring brought some relief but there was then a plan discovered to effect the queen's escape by night through a window. The immediate result of this was a crackdown: her household was disarmed (most well-to-do men carried a knife or dagger as part of their normal dress) and a 9 p.m. to 6 a.m. curfew was imposed on them.[12]

As an added measure the numbers of her court were reduced again, the instruction being to get as near to thirty as possible. Mary's tearful protestations were enough to produce some lenient dealings by the earl, however, and thirty-nine were allowed to stay. The alarm had not passed, however, and despite the fact that Mary continued to be regularly ill through 1571, the guard on her was doubled to forty, including the introduction of *arquebusiers*. The guard was charged with clearing corridors and rooms around the castle ahead of her progress, simply to restrict her association with any who were not in her court.[13]

In October her court was further reduced and a guard placed on all her retainers, putting the entire court into house arrest. In the midst of her illness Mary's physician complained that he had little with which to treat her and that he was reduced to being a doctor in name only.[14]

At about this time the Earl of Shrewsbury went to the royal court, summoned to preside over the forthcoming trial of the Duke of Norfolk, and Mary was provided with a substitute jailer, Sir Ralph Sadler, of whom she was very wary, perhaps fearing that he had prying intentions, which of course was one of his jobs. He had sat as judge at her first tribunal while she was still at Bolton. Sadler too seemed wary, perhaps overawed. He changed the watch on her regularly and precisely and reported her moods and her movements. She apparently met regularly with the countess but also spent a lot of time on her own in her quarters, fasting and praying, particularly while she knew the Catholic Duke of Norfolk stood trial for treason, and her devotions were directed towards a successful outcome for him. Neither is surprising in a particularly religious age, but the fasting may have been more convenient for a woman whose stomach trouble hardly left her. When Shrewsbury himself pronounced a sentence of death on Norfolk, he is said to have done so in tears, for he respected and admired the man. The effect on Mary, who had been mooted as the one and only prospective wife to the aspirant and treacherous duke, was just as profound. As to her jailer, Sadler was bored by it all, describing his time as 'an idle life'. Mary made the odd foray outside, under strong guard, memorably expressing delight at going out in the snow. Some correspondence probably made it in or out despite Sadler, for some we know was foiled when a bag with a false bottom was discovered.

The year 1572 saw the return of Mary's sickness, which recent historians have suggested might have been the debilitating porphyria. The cold was preying upon her and she complained of having insufficient clothes. Nevertheless she was able to procure and send to Elizabeth gifts of satin, taffeta and linen, no doubt finely embroidered in her own hand. That year also saw her mood darken, after the gloom of Norfolk's execution. She was said to be melancholic and she began to complain bitterly of the wrongs done to her in her imprisonment. Her estate may have been eased by a legacy given to her by Norfolk before his execution, a potential 40,000 crowns. She denied it, but it was half-hearted.

In April 1573 she was moved from Sheffield Castle to Sheffield Lodge and then Chatsworth House, ostensibly to cleanse her apartments. Although such housekeeping was probably necessary, it was also a good excuse to rummage mercilessly and find all the nooks, crannies and hiding places for her ciphers and illicit correspondence. Although that summer saw her health improve, she asked to visit Buxton to take the waters. There she bathed in herbs in the late summer and stayed upwards of five weeks, hoping to gain longer-term relief from her pain. Lord Burghley is said to have joined her for relief of arthritis he felt in his hands, which enraged Elizabeth no end. The entire village was closed to strangers during her visit. From there she went back to Sheffield Castle in the autumn.[15]

1573 brought alarm to the court as it was riven by an outbreak of measles that raged through April and May, forcing her removal to Sheffield Lodge for that period.

There is some suggestion that Mary's physician had been withdrawn at this period since she praised her chief cook for his vigilance of her food (she feared poisoning). Apparently denied an apothecary, her cook made up all her medicines for her, although she lamented she could get neither *terra sigillata* nor unicorn's horn. She may not have thought so, but she may have been better off without them.

After seven years Mary could no longer embroider her finances – they were now threadbare. Her dowry from France had all been spent on her cause in Scotland and it is against this growing penury that she may be seen commissioning painted miniatures of herself, to be given as presents to drum up support.[16]

The boredom of the passing years must have been crushing. For long periods Mary hardly figures in documents, most particularly the later 1570s, in danger of being forgotten. In 1575 her upkeep was drastically reduced, from £52 to £30 a week. This was a stricture forced by the Crown on the Earl of Shrewsbury, who protested, but to no avail. She seems to have had meat to spare, however, as she kept three spaniels and two bloodhounds, gifts from the well-meaning earl. Eventually, although very fond of them, she sent them to a friend as a gift, perhaps unable to keep them in the confines of her quarters.[17]

From the middle of June 1576, Mary spent another month at Buxton, hoping from intelligence that she might meet Elizabeth there, but in vain. Her hopes were gradually being dashed in all quarters. France, her greatest ally, was becoming less and less helpful. The French government envoy heard that she was almost continually ill, spending most of her time, whether because of illness or design, in her own quarters. She was in fact now afflicted with a hard, swollen and distended stomach and was in constant pain. In the autumn of 1578, despite plague in the capital, the Countess of Shrewsbury went to court on her husband's behalf to ask the queen to increase their allowance for Mary's upkeep. Shrewsbury estimated that he was spending £1,000 a year over the state allowance on wine, spices and fuel from his own pocket. It is assumed that Elizabeth questioned the countess in detail concerning Mary's health and appearance.

Mary went to Buxton again in 1580 for the waters but this time it did her more harm than good, as while waiting to begin her journey her horse threw her and she landed badly. She hurt her back and was battered and bruised for some time. This visit to Buxton saw her still confined, denied the relative freedom of previous occasions. Ironically this may have been of benefit as her entire court came down with a nasty bug while they were there. Seemingly only Mary escaped it.[18]

Her slowly failing health was a source of constant worry to Mary, who wrote in early 1581 of her weak and feeble state; she bemoaned the poor quality of her food and that she was fed bad meat. Her digestion could ill afford this and it was noted at the time that 'her left side and thigh have long been ill and to ease the pain she is forced to use continually medicines and poultices',[19] presumably not including unicorn's horn. She was nevertheless able to visit Chatsworth again in this year, when it was noted that her hair had by now gone grey; she was thirty-eight.[20] From 1576 onwards she was visited less and less by the Earl and Countess of Shrewsbury and the increasing isolation cannot have helped her growing introspection, forced more and more to while away the hours in needlework.

As the winter of 1581 set in, Mary's health worsened enough to cause concern to both her and Shrewsbury's doctors. Robert Beale, clerk to the Privy Council was sent to assess the situation. Warned of Mary's apparent deviousness, he entered her bedchamber in the dark and unannounced. He was met by her ladies-in-waiting, sobbing as they recounted her complaints. Upon Beale's report to court, Elizabeth agreed to relax Mary's confinement, approving a request to take further exercise. As a result, Mary's health improved somewhat.

In June 1582 she went to Buxton again while her quarters were cleaned and an inventory taken, while the following year she was allowed to visit Worksop Manor, where she was allowed to walk in Sherwood Forest. Exercise was now no longer easy and she too now drew attention to the pain she was suffering in her legs and hips. She was said to have a waxy complexion and her features were now puffed up. Despite becoming such a sad figure, and having nothing to recommend her to him but her claim to England's throne, Mary was briefly linked with an apparently secret plan to marry Philip of Spain in a Catholic alliance that would have undermined the Crown and government. To discredit her (and scotch any plans, real or imagined) her reputation was compromised by rumours of a love child with the Earl of Shrewsbury. Believed in some quarters, it went so far as the countess and her sons being called to court to state categorically that Mary had borne no love child while in captivity.[21] Despite being incarcerated, Mary had the power to unsettle the entire government.

In 1584 Queen Elizabeth released the Shrewsburys from their increasingly onerous task, intending to move Mary to Melbourne in Derbyshire. In July she was at Buxton again for her last visit there. She was indeed moved, but not to Melbourne. Instead it was back to South Wingfield with Ralph Sadler again, to whom Mary was indifferent. The Earl of Shrewsbury finally took his leave. There had been hardly any let-up in the pressure to be exerted upon Mary. Sadler's letter of appointment from Elizabeth requires him to keep his charge secure and avoid unnecessary exposure in public. She was 'not permitted to ride farre abroad but onely suffered on foot or in a coache to take ayre and use some such exercise neere the howse where she shall lye'.[22]

The despised Tutbury beckoned once more. It was ready for her in December 1584 although there was still some delay. Ralph Sadler declared to the Crown that Wingfield contained 210 persons, of whom 150 were guards-cum-attendants. Of these forty to fifty were trained soldiers. Fifteen or sixteen guarded her nightly. Her court stood at forty-eight and she had only the same two chambers to herself. Although still technically a queen (in reality her son was King of Scotland), at forty-one she had nothing but her clothing and this was now said to be worn out. The hours of sunlight she spent mainly at her needlework or religious devotions. She remained in constant pain and discomfort. Mary, it seemed, had reached rock bottom.[23]

Still the screw was tightened further. With the inevitable flow of wine and merriment that Christmas brought, Robert Dudley, Earl of Leicester, wrote on Elizabeth's behalf to Sir Francis Walsingham, Sadler's boss, to restrict Mary's court and to 'give styckt order to his servants that they should have no conference with the Queen of Scottes folks, spetyally pryvatly'.[24]

News of Mary's declining health must have reached Elizabeth that Christmas since she now wrote suddenly to Sadler, requiring him 'to order the remove as that yt maie not be dangerous or prejudityall to her health'. The letter carried a warning in the queen's own handwriting that, in guarding her, Sadler should 'use but olde trust and new diligence'.[25]

Inventories were taken at this time, which relate the goods transferred from Wingfield to Tutbury in 1585 for Mary's use: damask tablecloths and napkins, silver flagons, bowls, basins and ewers. Another records hangings, tapestries, Turkish carpets, beds and bolsters, chairs, cushions of cloth of gold, stools, footstools, sheets and pillowcases being sent from the Tower of London.[26]

Early in the New Year Sadler received detailed instructions on the mode of Mary's custody at Tutbury. The household was to be reduced to forty by removing mothers with young children but so too was the guard to be reduced to thirty. As a check and balance Sadler was to mount regular but unannounced spot searches throughout the castle 'so as all strangers to be found in that serche maie be forthecoming'.[27] Only a week later William Cecil, Lord Burghley, informed Sadler, on the queen's orders, that the cost of Mary's upkeep had to be reduced to under £1,500 a year, a target which Cecil himself thought impossible.[28]

It was not long, however, before worrying reports reached Elizabeth of an unacceptable leniency creeping into Sadler's dealings with Mary, relaxing the regime which had been that of the Earl of Shrewsbury, and Walsingham wrote of her displeasure.[29] In his reply Sadler was a little incredulous, believing his regime to be correct. However, perhaps fearing some taint to his own integrity or allegiance, he went on to state that he wished the task could be given to someone else as he was weary of it.

That did the trick and before a month was out Elizabeth sent word to Sadler that he was relieved of his burden.[30] He was replaced by Sir Amyas Paulet. By the end of the year Mary was moved again, although not far. In what might have been seen by some as one of the regular cleansings of Tutbury, she was sent to the old thirteenth-century fortress of Chartley Castle, also in Staffordshire. Here, although the castle was approaching the end of its useful days, there were sufficient lodgings between it and the replacement manor house next door to accommodate both Mary's court and the troops guarding her. It was also a more deliberately open and relaxed place where Mary might drop her guard.

Whether as a result of her removal from Tutbury or a change of regime at Chartley, the stay was to be brief and stormy. Here she became embroiled in a plot to assassinate Elizabeth. Now known to history as the Babington Plot, named after one Anthony Babington, who as a young boy of ten was a page to the Earl of Shrewsbury at Chatsworth and Sheffield and would have come into regular contact with Mary. Popular at court, Babington had now become involved with other prominent Catholics who had designs on freeing Mary.

At around this time Walsingham's spies apprehended one Robert Gifford, who confessed to knowing of a plot to assassinate Elizabeth and place Mary on the throne. Turned double agent, Gifford became Walsingham's eyes and ears at Chartley, and Mary responded, swallowing the bait hook, line and sinker. In July Walsingham had a letter of disinformation sent secretly via Gifford to entrap Mary, by means of a watertight container concealed in a barrel. In her reply she accepted that England would have to be invaded by Spain and that Elizabeth would have to be assassinated so that she herself could be freed.

On 11 August, Mary was allowed to hunt at Tixall, 5 miles from Chartley. Sighting a band of horsemen, led by the queen's emissary, Mary was told that her part in the conspiracy had been exposed. She was escorted on to Tixall Castle where she was placed in isolation for two weeks. On her return to Chartley her rooms were in disarray after a particularly thorough search. Sufficient incriminating materials were found to ensure Mary's guilt in any forthcoming trial.

Matters moved swiftly thereafter. With Mary soon under stricter guard at Chartley, Lord Burghley wrote from Windsor on 16 September 1586 that Mary should be taken to Fotheringhay Castle in north-east Northamptonshire by 28 September, to be joined by 5 October by the lords who would hear the case.[31] Mary's trial took place there on 14/15 October; she was charged with attempting to usurp the English crown and seeking Elizabeth's death. Although on the second day Mary defended herself with great courage, her part in the plot was beyond doubt. Ten days later in the Star Chamber in London, Mary's judges delivered their guilty verdict.

As a former fortress of the kings of Scotland (as earls of Huntingdon), Fotheringhay may have been seen as offering Mary some brief crumb of comfort. She was probably confined in the keep, at the time called 'the Fetterlocks'. In plan this probably resembled a hollow ring, with a small, round court with a well in the centre.[32] Whether she enjoyed any liberty through the cold winter of 1586/7 is a moot point. Fotheringhay was – and remains – a most pleasant place of honey-coloured stone houses, dominated by the stately collegiate church by the languid River Nene, its vole-frequented banks fringed by rushes and dipped by kingfishers, its waters disturbed only by the wash of a passing boat and the wakes of families of waterfowl.

Ironically the Earl of Shrewsbury was given the onerous task of telling Mary the outcome of the trial and the sentence passed, a foregone conclusion. The world remembers Mary going to the scaffold on 9 February 1587 in the courtyard of the castle; to all intents and purposes it was hereditary Scots soil, but ringed all about by England. The Earl of Shrewsbury is said to have wept openly at her execution.

Only the motte and the earthworks of the baileys on which Fotheringhay stood remain today. A huge chunk of shattered masonry lies at the foot of the motte, cradled by wild flowers. It is an exceedingly green and beautiful place today, frequented by picnickers seeking peace and solitude, and anglers glad of the silence and the stillness.

James I, uniting England and Scotland in 1603, had the castle destroyed in an embittered but vain attempt to erase the memory of his mother's demise. However, her powerless passage through so many lives across England and the aspirations of her Catholic faith continue to ensure her legacy. In her end was her beginning; Mary was always far more than just any captive.

7

INTRIGUE & THE WOULD-BE ESCAPER

CHARLES I IN ENGLAND (1646–48)

After the decisive Battle of Naseby ended the English Civil War in 1645, any viable royalist cause of the imperious Charles I against his detractors in Parliament was effectively lost. While considerable support for the king could still be found, it was scattered, disjointed and unable to coalesce into a viable force to continue the Civil War in the military terms which had characterised the period 1642–5 and pockets of support were reduced to merely brigandage. Charles was at the mercy of Parliament whose victorious army was at best cock-a-hoop but ill directed, at worst bored and dangerously unpaid.

By April 1646 Charles decided to either treat with the Scots and seek terms with them or flee overseas and exile, probably to France where he would join the queen, Henrietta Maria, in Paris (the Prince of Wales was travelling via Jersey and St Malo to Paris while the other royal children were at St James's Palace). While early negotiations with the Scots went on, Charles moved from Middlesex to Norfolk and the East Coast, mainly in a regular change of disguises, getting ready to flee. At Downham Market he was almost recognised at the White Swan Inn because of his clergyman's clothes. While there, he heard the news that the Scots would keep him safe and so plans to flee out of King's Lynn were abandoned and he headed through Cambridgeshire and the Fens, still travelling incognito until he met his Scots friends at Southwell, Nottinghamshire. A few days later his negotiations persuaded his last remaining strongholds of nearby Newark and later Oxford, the former royalist wartime capital, to surrender and their garrisons marched out. Meanwhile he was moved to Newcastle upon Tyne by his Scots friends, who preached at him all the way.

In the simplest of terms he was attempting to agree with them to give him asylum against his enemies in Parliament.

At Newcastle the king was said to be bored and lonely and was contemplating escape. He wrote to the queen to ask her opinion. His mood deteriorated, and he only managed to divert himself by playing chess and golf. Many said he appeared sullen as he became depressed. Newcastle was clearly a safe distance from the asylum he sought. The dilatory nature of Scots negotiations was alarming and it became clear that they were unconvinced by his pleas. Meanwhile Parliament, as part of their negotiations with the Scots, looked around for a 'safe house' for Charles 'where he can stay in honour and safety, attended as Parliament may decide'.[1] Internal exile by any other name. It was perhaps not yet outright imprisonment.

His so-called new place of honour and safety was in fact well known to him already, and the thought was not displeasing. Holdenby House (pronounced Holmby) in Northamptonshire was already a royal residence and Charles had spent many happy days there in his youth. It was a magnificent, showy palace, built by the Lord Chancellor, Sir Christopher Hatton I, specifically to honour Queen Elizabeth I.

Their journey from Newcastle took eight days and everywhere they stopped crowds flocked to see the king, although none tried to check or interfere with the troops who were guarding him.[2] They knew he was coming as his progress was carefully stage-managed, and his overnight lodgings vetted. He was accompanied by only those whose politics had passed muster. At Holdenby he drew a large crowd who came to welcome him. The house had been prepared for his arrival by his servant to the wardrobe and his politically selected court had been assembled around him from Newcastle, including a number of Northamptonshire men.[3]

Life at Holdenby quickly settled down to a routine, during which Charles maintained a grace and elegance under considerable pressure. He was a pious man and his religious devotions were to the fore, although he was denied his own ministers in favour of appointed men trusted by Parliament. He would hear them preach all day on Sunday before taking himself off for his private devotions. During the week he spent two to three hours at prayer and Bible reading. After meals, at which the king always insisted on saying grace personally, he played chess with the parliamentary commissioners who were in charge of his custody, being not ill disposed towards either of them.

Charles had always enjoyed sports and one thing Holdenby lacked was a bowling green. Such grass-plats are not created overnight and so the king was allowed to travel to neighbouring Harrowden, where Lord Vaux maintained a green amid pleasing gardens and places to walk and seek diversions in stimulating surroundings. Even nearer was Althorpe, where Lord Spencer also played a mean end! The latter was only 3 miles away, so became a regular haunt, and between the two, this love of bowls and his innate capacity for intrigue indirectly led to a tightening of security around him.

In April Charles was on his way to Harrowden for just such a game, and passed over a bridge where a royalist agent, a Major Boswell, waited in disguise.[4] He stopped the king, possibly quite rudely, and took the opportunity to pass him a packet of letters from the queen, who was in exile at the French court in Paris. The attempt was crude although the letters got through. Boswell was however arrested and later suffered for his subterfuge. Shortly afterwards an unknown woman was also arrested for apparently trying to pass a packet to the king.

The effect was immediate. Guards around the king were doubled, and he was rarely alone, such that even the Dutch ambassador had to be received by the king before a parliamentary commissioner. The freshly outraged Charles wrote to Parliament complaining of his treatment – he had been complaining for some time; Parliament, of course, remained divided as to what to do with Charles, so consensus to get any relaxation of his conditions was impossible.

Parliament's new, harsher regime was to strip the king of more trappings of privilege. All but two of his household servants were dismissed, the exceptions being two grooms to his bed chamber. All were ceremonially allowed to depart one evening after dinner and there were genuine tears. The king, overcome, took to his bed early.[5]

Despite the tightening of Parliament's grip, Charles's personal guards, the parliamentary commissioners, were by no means ill disposed towards him. Many were very friendly, and in time he came to trust them to an extent, not least James Harrington and Thomas Herbert, the former a political theorist who strongly espoused the ideas of a commonwealth, the latter a well-travelled diplomat. Nonetheless both were spies, but the king liked them. Another, Major General Browne, the king genuinely liked and would often choose him as his walking companion in the gardens at Holdenby. Others kept a respectful distance.

During the spring the king's children were sent to spend the summer at Hampton Court. They were under house arrest but did not for the moment share their father's incarceration. The queen was at Fontainebleau and at St Germain with the French court, urging her husband to accept whatever terms he was offered. At the same time Parliament finally replied to Charles's regular requests for his own chaplains – they refused. Charles wrote to Parliament complaining of this treatment.[6]

The daily routine at Holdenby, although perhaps increasingly restricted, came to a sudden and unexpected end in June. Throughout the winter and spring the army had remained under arms but was increasingly restive, many having not been paid for months and others unhappy about rumours of their disbandment. Elements of the army had decided to act on their own accord and the night of 3/4 June proved to be what amounted to a military coup.

On 3 June Charles was bowling as usual at Althorpe, when news arrived (presumably from his own spies or those of his commissioners) of an unofficial body of horsemen on its way to Holdenby. Charles and his party rushed back there, but found no one and nothing untoward and the household retired as usual. However, at midnight a ragtag body of fifty assorted cavalry troopers under a young subaltern and cornet, George Joyce, cantered into the courtyard in a clatter of hooves and shouts, come to take the king into their protective custody.[7] Most of the commissioners fled and a brief stand-off ensued, only ended when Charles's guards and the troopers began to fraternise.

Charles was asleep in his chambers and Joyce was able to gain entry via a servants' back stair to the royal bedchamber, pistol in hand, loaded and cocked. He refused to be disarmed and the atmosphere was electric as he hammered on the king's bedroom door and demanded entrance. The king, quickly out of bed and half-dressed, refused to see him and despite a heated exchange through the locked door, Joyce was persuaded that he would not gain entry until morning. He retired for a few hours to wait.

Come morning the situation, less tense perhaps but no less momentous, was resolved. Joyce and two others were let into the king's bedroom, hats off in a polite gesture, but all three with pistols loaded and cocked, less politely. When Charles asked by what authority Joyce had come, he brandished his pistol as his answer.[8] Charles was allowed to take some breakfast but was said to have thought he was done for, but retaining some decorum, chose to inspect his new guard outside Holdenby. He flattered them for their audacity and spirit. This was a military coup and Charles was once more a pawn, a bystander in his own story.

The cavalry took him to Newmarket in Suffolk, stopping at the houses of supporters, where he was well received. Through June he was in East Anglia where he met army commanders one by one. The army was seething with malcontents and there were numerous spokesmen for small contingents. The very fact that some now dealt directly with the king without the sanction of Parliament, put their careers (and lives) on the line. London was in a panic as in early July Charles headed for the capital, for some time unclear whether it would be Hampton Court or Syon House. Parliament, seeking to placate him, sent him three sumptuously appointed coaches for his journey. He eventually settled at Hampton Court, from where he visited his children at Syon House in August. He remained around London for a couple of months, gathering information and intelligence, before rumours of impending imprisonment and even murder reached his ears.

Unwilling to panic he retired early to his apartments at Hampton Court on 11 November, skipping his evening meal. There he wrote three letters (or sent out three letters he had already written – to his guard, to the commissioners and to the army). A fourth, unsigned, warned of a plot against him. That he took his leave early aroused no suspicions and while Charles escaped through the gardens, it was many hours before his guards discovered his absence.

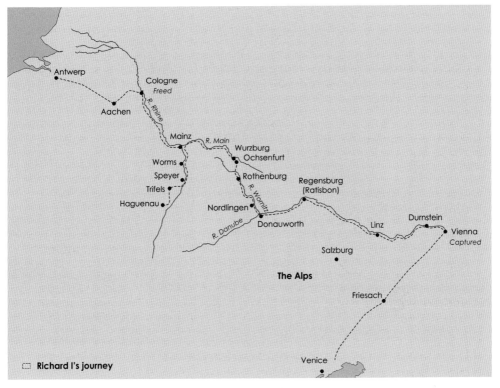

1 Map of the captive journey of Richard I. (Amir Bassir)

Antwerp
Cologne
Freed
Aachen
R. Rhine
Mainz
R. Main
Wurzburg
Ochsenfurt
Worms
Speyer
Rothenburg
Trifels
R. Wornitz
Regensburg
(Ratisbon)
Haguenau
Nordlingen
R. Danube
Donauworth
Durnstein
Linz
Vienna
Captured
Salzburg
The Alps
Friesach
Richard I's journey
Venice

2 The view east along the Danube from Dürnstein Castle, Austria (1989).

3 View of Dürnstein Castle (Austria) from the Danube (1989).

4 Richard the Lionheart's river journeys: the Danube at Ottensheim, 10 km west of Linz (2011).

5 The River Main crossing near Ochsenfurt (Würzburg) (1990).

6 Hertford Castle, Jean II's most comfortable abode outside London (2011).

Above: 7 St Leonard's church, Bengeo (2011).

Left: 8 St Albans Abbey, Hertfordshire (2011): Jean II found solace and friendship here.

Opposite: 9 Guesthouse, St Albans Abbey (2011).

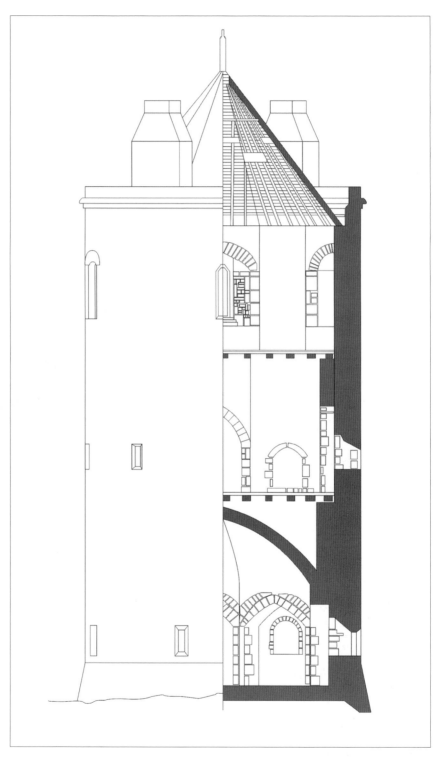

10 Surviving tower of Somerton Castle, Lincolnshire. (Amir Bassir, after a nineteenth-century drawing)

Right: 11 The windswept landscape of Somerton, Lincolnshire (2011).

Below: 12 Boothby Graffoe church, near Somerton, Lincolnshire (2011).

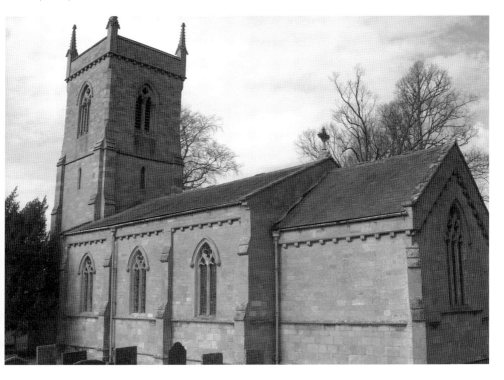

Left: 13 Berkhamsted Castle,
Hertfordshire: the keep earthworks
(2011).

Below: 14 The Tower of London,
drawn in the seventeenth century.
(*Vetusta monumenta* (1815):
thanks to Joe Prentice)

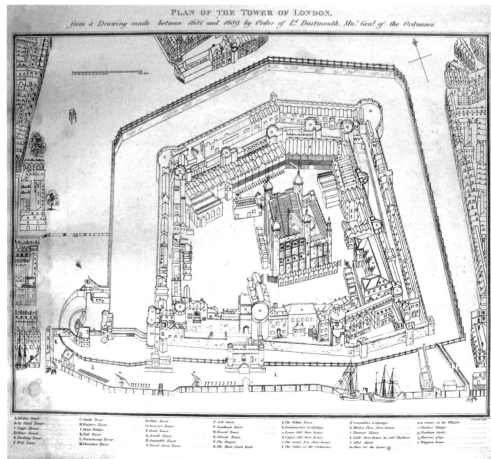

PLAN OF THE TOWER OF LONDON,
from a Drawing made between 1681 and 1689, by Order of L.ᵈ Dartmouth, Ma.ʳ Gen.ˡ of the Ordnance.

15 Pontefract Castle, West Yorkshire: the keep (2012).

16 Fotheringhay, Northamptonshire (2006): the castle was a prison of Charles of Orleans and venue of Mary, Queen of Scots's trial and execution. The Duke of York, killed at Agincourt, was buried in the church.

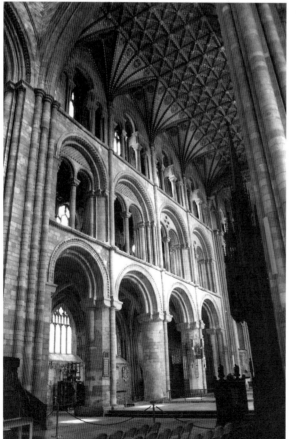

Above: 17 Bolingbroke Castle, Lincolnshire (2008).

Left: 18 Peterborough Abbey (now Cathedral, 2009): it was here that Charles, Duke of Orleans, was allowed to meet his younger brother, who was being held nearby at Maxey.

19 House in Damme, West Flanders, Belgium: the wedding venue of Margaret of York and Charles the Bold (2010).

20 Edward IV. (Reproduced courtesy of the National Portrait Gallery, London)

Left: 21 Bruges, Flanders, Belgium (2010): the Marshal Gate. Medieval Bruges was perhaps the most defensible city opposite England in which to set up a court in exile.

Below: 22 Bruges: the Gruuthuse Palace (2009). Edward IV was lodged here in the finest cultured surroundings.

Above: 23 The English
House, Bruges, West
Flanders, Belgium (2010).

Right: 24 St Anne's church,
Bruges, West Flanders,
Belgium (2010).

25 The canal from Bruges to Damme (2010). Edward IV was forced to walk the 7 km to the inland port by crowds of boats loaded with well-wishers at Bruges.

South View.

26 The Tower of London, drawn in the seventeenth century. (*Vetusta monumenta* (1815): thanks to Joe Prentice)

Right: 27 Henry VII.
(Reproduced courtesy of the
National Portrait Gallery,
London)

Below: 28 Nantes, Loire
Atlantique, France: The Ducal
Palace (2007).

29 Largoët Castle, Morbihan, Brittany: prison of Henry Tudor (2010).

30 Largoët, also known as Elven Towers, Morbihan, France (2010).

31 Vannes, Morbihan, Brittany (2005): here Henry Tudor breathed more easily, fell in love and planned his return to Wales.

32 Suscinio, Morbihan, Brittany (2005): hunting parties from Duke Francis's fabulous hunting lodge were a regular treat for Henry and Jasper Tudor while at nearby Vannes.

33 Mary, Queen of Scots. (Reproduced courtesy of the National Portrait Gallery, London)

Right: 34 Tutbury Castle, Staffordshire: the gatehouse (2012).

Below: 35 South Wingfield Manor, Derbyshire (2011): Mary, Queen of Scots was moved here both for her health and for her previous lodgings to be 'cleaned'.

36 St Mary's Hall, Coventry (2012).

Right: 37
Tutbury Castle,
Staffordshire:
apartments (2012).

Below: 38
Chartley Castle,
Staffordshire
(1997).

39 Fotheringhay Castle, Northamptonshire (2012).

Right: 40 Charles I.
(Reproduced courtesy of the
National Portrait Gallery,
London)

Below: 41 Holdenby House,
Northamptonshire (2012): first
prison of Charles I.

Above: 42 Hurst Castle, Hampshire: seaward side (2012).

Opposite: 43 Hurst Castle, Hampshire: the polygonal tower at its core (2012).

Left: 44 Charles II. (Reproduced courtesy of the National Portrait Gallery, London)

45 Courtyard at the home of Thomas Preston, Bruges, West Flanders, Belgium (2010).

46 The Casselberg, Bruges, West Flanders, Belgium (2010).

47 Bruges, Flanders, Belgium (2009): the Green Quay. Charles, like Edward IV before him, threw himself into the civic life of this welcoming city.

48 Bruges, St George's Archers' Guild Hall (2010): Charles was honoured with membership by the guild. In the distance is the church of the English Carmelites where Lady Helen Bedingfield, the prioress, was a staunch royalist.

Left: 49 Edward Hyde, Earl of Clarendon. (Courtesy of the National Portrait Gallery)

Below: 50 Bruges, Flanders, Belgium (2009): Kruispoort. Charles II's first and last sights of this magnificent city were of its strong defences.

51 Corfe Castle, Dorset (2008): here Eleanor of Brittany whiled away her childbearing years in guarded isolation, her claim to Brittany too strong to allow her to be set free.

52 Château Gaillard (2003): David II of Scotland and his queen were given the castle as their home by the King of France.

53 Odiham Castle, Hampshire (2012).

54 Pontefract Castle, West Yorkshire: chapel ruins (2012).

55 Rhuddlan Castle, Wales (2007): like Caernarfon and Conwy, the castle was prison to French captives after the battles of Agincourt and Harfleur.

56 Conwy Castle, Wales (2007).

57 Caernarfon Castle, Wales (2007): this was the favoured prison after the battles of Agincourt and Harfleur.

By early December word of the king's escape had spread far and wide. Far from being at liberty, he was the most wanted man in England when as early as 28 November Venetian spies reported that he had fetched up on the Isle of Wight. That Parliament also knew quickly was clear. His place of refuge, Carisbrooke Castle, was quickly to become his next prison. Those same spies stated that the people of the island welcomed him generously and maintained him by means of a voluntary tax. However, the governor was requested by Parliament to arrest Charles and guards were posted all around the island by Christmas 1647.[9]

As his honoured guest, the governor could not in integrity arrest the king, but he did promise his safety, which was tantamount to imprisonment. The king was joined by some of his servants and he spent his spare time in hunting and was afforded some liberty. However, he remained under constant guard. News of his new abode only reached Henrietta Maria in Paris the following month. She was said to be very aggrieved. The story which was soon making its way across the Continent was not one to warm her heart. Spies reported that the conditions of Charles's stay were quickly made greatly more stringent, despite the fact that when he arrived the castle garrison had been only a dozen old men. He was soon restricted to two rooms in the castle and his servants were reduced to only two; he was left to his library and his bowls. Even his chaplains were taken away although he struck up a friendship with the castle chaplain.[10] The island was blockaded by a squadron of eight warships. By February his door was guarded round the clock and he was watched constantly. He still had his library with him and in the castle barbican the governor had a bowling green laid out for him and a summer-house erected for him to retire to and to write in during the day as the spring weather improved.[11]

The need for Charles to lead the royalist cause was paramount and a bold plan was hatched. It was intended that Charles should escape by removing a piece of the ceiling and climbing up to emerge in a part of the castle that was not guarded and from there make his escape.[12] The plan was said to have come from the king's tailor, a Mr Murray, but the plan was discovered and came to nothing. The effect was to rebound on him as his apartments were searched and the castle governor even scuffled with him, possibly as the search uncovered a chink in the panelling that was used to house secret notes, the presence or absence of which was indicated by the way in which a hanging on the wall was arranged.[13] He was moved to new, more spartan apartments where he could be better watched.

The news of his harsh conditions continued to be leaked by the Venetians with some alacrity, anxious to portray his state as a victim as a Commonwealth-run England was aiding the Turks against Venice. They were naturally very keen to support Charles who might offer some reversal of the

English position were he to regain power. However in the middle of March they reported back that he no longer had a voice, nor were his despatches getting out, proving that the search by Colonel Hammond, the governor, had been successful. In London the situation was deteriorating and civil riots ensued, brutally put down with cavalry. That month the brief Second Civil War began, the king entirely on the sidelines there on the Isle of Wight.

Perhaps in response to the worsening situation, another plot was hatched to spring Charles from Carisbrooke. He was to escape over the wall in the dead of night by rope from a pre-arranged window. The date 20 March was set for the act but, in a remarkably simplistic and amateurish plot, the king got stuck between the bars on his window. He groaned audibly at the time. It was bizarrely undignified for the former Head of State.[14] Unperturbed they tried a similar attempt on 1 May but this too was discovered, because of captured ciphered documents, before it could be put into action.[15] The king's apartments were quickly searched again and, although he was not moved again, building work was put in hand to guard his windows and further ensure his safe keeping.

In the middle of June, news leaked out that Charles for a brief period had indeed escaped from the castle and was at liberty on the island. He was soon recaptured and no details of how he made his escape are known. There were numerous movements during this summer, as the young Duke of York escaped from Hampton Court and made his way to Holland by fishing boat. The Prince of Wales, later Charles II, was agitating from France and Holland, looking to turn the Scots into a viable opposition.

Throughout the summer the activities of the Prince of Wales along the south coast gave increasing cause for concern. He was raiding and plundering merchant shipping and even approached the Isle of Wight at Yarmouth, although he could not land. England began to fear a royalist blockade, although this was surely unfounded as the Prince of Wales had only a dozen ships or so. In any case as the autumn wore on supplies dwindled, and with winter storms approaching, the fleet broke up and the raiding came to an end.[16] However, the vulnerability of Charles on the Isle of Wight was exposed and plans were put in hand to move him. The move took place on 1 December 1648 and was said by all to have involved a great deal of casual violence, the king being taken as a stopgap measure to Hurst Castle, a (by comparison) pokey Henrician shore fort on the nearby Hampshire coast looking out at the Needles.[17]

Here the governor was a fearsome, grim-faced man with wild, hirsute looks who went around armed to the teeth. Charles was said to have quickly won him over and he was afforded a degree of freedom and took regular walks on the Solent-shifted shingle that rings the fort. However, the interior conditions could not be improved. This was a purpose-built artillery fort of the 1540s with no concessions possible to either regal living or even lesser comforts. He was in cramped quarters and at midday in midwinter his two rooms needed candles in order to see. At night his bedchamber continued to be lit by a wax lamp in a silver basin, the last trapping of his regal position. Everything stank of seaweed and the nearby salt marshes.[18] Only two retainers, Herbert and Harrington, now attended him.

Hurst has since Charles's day been vastly increased in size, due to its continued strategic location. Napoleonic-era, Victorian and twentieth-century additions have smothered the sixteenth-century core, but its location remains isolated. It remains accessed via a narrow spit of shingle that bars the racing currents of the Solent to south and west and links it to the mainland, or it can be approached by a regular and very pleasant water taxi from the nearby Keyhaven across a glassy lagoon in the lee of the shingle spit. Today it is home to many dozen yachts and pleasure craft and is a joy.

The isolation was not to last long, however, and by Christmas 1648 Charles was taken to Windsor Castle where he would prepare for his trial. Mr Herbert remained with him throughout, although Harrington now refused to go further, disgusted at the increasingly insulting behaviour to which Charles was subjected. From Windsor he was taken to St James's Palace, and although both were royal palaces, together they represented his last stops. From St James's and Whitehall, it was just a short walk to the scaffold on 30 January 1649, condemned by a court whose legitimacy he refused to acknowledge. He was forty-eight years old, but looked older, his hair and beard turned grey by his captivity.

While held captive, he had given some of his time to writing, and within a short time his supporters – and there were still very many – published these memoirs. He had a number of reflections to make. On his first move to Holdenby he noted wryly, 'Well may I change my keepers and prison, but not my captive state.' Later, concerning Carisbrooke, he was no less fatalistic, perhaps remembering the experiences of his grandmother, Mary, Queen of Scots, saying, 'I know there are but few steps between the prisons and graves of princes.'[19]

He did not bear captivity well. It weighed heavily upon him, not eased by the fruitless escape attempts. His letters that made it out, even those to his children, spoke of him being 'out of humour' and with little to say.[20] It was, all in all, a melancholy experience, which all but crushed his spirit, if not his defiance.

He expected not to survive and wrote, 'Indeed they have left me but little of life, and only the husk and shell, as it were, which their further malice and cruelty can take from me; having bereaved me of all those worldly comforts for which life itself seems desirable to men.'[21]

His words are perhaps spoken for all prisoners without hope of parole or release in any age.

8

OUTSTAYING ONE'S WELCOME

PRINCE CHARLES (CHARLES II) IN BRUGES (1656–58)

When he fled the Battle of Worcester in 1651, Prince Charles of England quit the realm, ending the so-called Second Civil War. He spent much of the next four years in relative poverty in Paris and Cologne, begging and borrowing whatever he could to keep his ambitions and those of his impoverished court alive.

As early as December 1655 it had become common knowledge in diplomatic circles that the penniless Charles was intending to leave Cologne, his credit well and truly exhausted there. He wished to go to Dunkirk, which his advisors thought too exposed, and was in discussion with the Spanish authorities in the Netherlands (Flanders) who were offering him asylum at Bruges.[1] Negotiations continued through the winter and in mid-March 1656 rumours abounded in London that Charles was about to leave Cologne, but no one was clear whether for Bruges or Brussels.[2] In fact he then based himself briefly in Brussels, but moved about somewhat, visiting his sister Mary, Princess of Orange, at Teilingen in Zeeland, where he caught up with intelligence from England. Spies soon caught up and she was apparently forced to send him away for his own safety, denying having news of him.[3] Returning to Brussels, he stayed for a further week or two, finalising negotiations with the Spanish authorities for his stay as their guest. He was attended by just a few servants, as his stay was to be incognito, in a vain hope that he would draw no attention.[4] However, his diplomatic front was somewhat misguided during this brief period since news was reported at Paris that would have dire repercussions for him later on. Charles's mother, the widowed queen, arrived at the French court and broke the 'news' that her son had decided to give up his Protestant, Church of England religion for the Roman Catholic faith, having decided that it was his only hope of regaining his kingdom (i.e., with Roman Catholic Continental help).[5] The Duke of Gloucester was said to be following suit while apparently Charles had already dismissed his Protestant servants in favour of Catholic ones.

This was most likely disinformation deliberately spread and designed to make his arrival in Spanish-controlled Flanders all the sweeter to his new hosts, for whom the prospect of a Roman Catholic England and their own part in its return to the spiritual fold, was a prospect to savour. However, these statements were also music to the ears of the Commonwealth authorities in England and only served to help disparate spiritual factions coalesce around their shared distaste of the Roman Church. Commonwealth agents continued to spread this same old story time and again and Charles's forward-thinking laissez-faire approach to the faith and religious observance of those around him would time and again be deliberately misrepresented by his enemies to his disadvantage in England, and eventually in Flanders too.

On 20 April 1656 the twenty-six-year-old Charles left Brussels with only a few chosen dignitaries, leaving a diplomatic community briefly worried as to his whereabouts and destination. On St George's Day 1656 he quietly entered the defences of Bruges on horseback. Others would join him in dribs and drabs and his 'incognito' court would eventually number 175 by the end of the summer, and that was only the official court members, who enjoyed daily access to the exiled king. One commentator has noted that the very idea he could live incognito was preposterous since there was no single residence which could accommodate the English court.[6] The quiet life he had promised to lead was clearly to be an illusion and the English would be all over Bruges.

Upon his arrival Charles made for the home of his friend Thomas Preston, Viscount of Tarach, who was a colonel in the service of Spain and a general of the Catholic league of Ireland. The house survives today as the former Hotel de Preston in the Oude Bourg at Bruges. There Charles settled while more appropriate quarters were made ready for his growing band to which was added, most notably, his sixteen-year-old brother, the Duke of Gloucester, in May. On the 22nd of that month they moved into an entire block of buildings called the Casselberg, on Hoogstraat, which had been cleared especially for them by its owners, the Lopez-Gallo family, and which survives today as one of the city's most sumptuous hotels, dominating its street frontage. Next door they also took over the House of Seven Towers, once an obvious and eponymous landmark. In fact these lodgings comprised an entire city block that stretched along Hoogstraat from side street to side street and down to the canal wharf at the rear, giving the court instant access to the two modes of transport and supply in Bruges: road and canal.[7]

News of Charles's arrival in Bruges quickly began to filter out. It reached England within days and spread rapidly. Francesco Giavarina, Venetian Secretary in England, passed it on to the doge in far-off Venice on 5 May.[8]

The effect of the news in England was electric. Giavarina noted that in England all letters from Flanders were inspected, and the addresses checked, to follow up on the intended recipients and their loyalties. They were opened and re-sealed. Not even diplomatic correspondence escaped. A month later and Giavarina speculated, not unreasonably, that Charles's proximity was provocative, designed to cause Cromwell and the Commonwealth state as much concern as possible, but he was perhaps unaware that the king had once actually preferred the even nearer Dunkirk as the new base for his court.[9] However, concern for Charles's safety had ruled that out.

During the summer and autumn the king settled down at Bruges, although he made regular visits back to Brussels, usually to try to get funds from the King of Spain, whose government ground very slowly indeed, leaving the already frugal English court even more impoverished. Small gifts of support did indeed come in, such as 1,000 florins from the English Mother Augustine and her Carmelite nuns at their Convent of Nazareth in Bruges.[10] However, for the moment there was no sign of the £6,000 a month for Charles and £3,000 to the Duke of Gloucester, which had been promised by the King of Spain, the absence of which grew more wearying with every week that passed.

Despite the funding situation, and perhaps partly because of it, Charles threw himself into the civic and religious life of Bruges. The court sought quickly to make allies of the city magistracy and the Bishop of Bruges.[11] On 11 June both he and the Duke of Gloucester were admitted into the Guild and Confraternity of St George. On 18 July the duke was admitted to that of St Sebastian, followed by Charles on 3 August. They were joined by General Middleton, Gilbert Talbot, William Keith and Edward Halsall, all prominent members of the court, although it was the duke's gift to the guild of an inscribed golden arrow which made the headlines, since theirs was a guild symbolised by shooting generally and the crossbow in particular.[12]

In the months following Charles's arrival the court continued to grow, exacerbating his precarious financial state. After months of dithering, James, Duke of York, arrived from Paris (later James II, 1685–8). He was noted as being bound for Bruges as early as May but his popularity at the French court had delayed him.[13] On 2 October 1656 all three brothers were admitted to the Bruges Brotherhood of the Arquebusiers of St Barbara.[14] They were joined in the city in November by their sister, Princess Mary, wife of William of Orange, who also arrived from Paris.

It is unusual to have detailed records of who comprised the court at any one time, but it may be because of the singular nature of Charles's that a 'census' of their names has come down to the present, published separately on both sides of the English Channel.[15] For the purposes of this book it is not their names which matter so much as the functions that were considered necessary for the government surrounding the 'king' to work effectively. For Charles in Bruges this comprised thirty-one principal persons: Lord Chancellor Marquis of Ormonde, the earls of Bristol, Norwich, and Rochester, all counsellors, the Bishop of Londonderry, seven lords, most of whom acted as privy counsellors, Secretary of State (Sir Edward Nicholas), a secretary, a judge, two chaplains, a colonel, a doctor, two clerks to the Privy Council, three grooms, a surgeon, clerk to the king's toilet (who monitored the king's health through his normal bodily functions), two pages, a keeper of the council chamber, a barber, three equerries, a coachman and 142 others, whose individual roles probably varied according to the needs of the king, comprising cooks, servants, cleaners, guards, errand boys etc. Twelve of the 'lesser' persons were also knights. To add to this, many of the higher-ranking individuals had their entire families with them in exile. Clearly the quarters set aside for Charles and his immediate family could not support all of these and many private properties across the city were pressed into service as lodgings.

However, this was not just becoming the entire English royal family and its entourage in residence, pursuing a round of diplomatic niceties, since the situation in England was forcing royalists of every status to flee the country. A ragtag trickle of troops who wavered in their allegiance to the Commonwealth defected; others in English service on the Continent, unpaid by Cromwell, joined the (equally unpaid) royalist troops opposed to them. Long into 1657 their numbers increased, on the whole not a good thing as the overburdened finances could not cope adequately, nor could the warmth of the reception they might receive. One of the later notable arrivals, Sir Richard Bellings, came in October 1657 in dire need of immediate surgery from a bullet in his jaw. The quality of care offered was not necessarily any good. Indeed the king's own physician at court, Tobias Whittaker, was also the author of the dubiously entitled *The Tree of Humane Life, or the Beloved of the Grape, Proving the Possibility of Maintaining Humane Life from Infancy to Extreme Old Age Without any Sicknesse by the Use of Wine*, published in 1638.[16] It is perhaps little wonder that the court quickly acquired a reputation for immorality and debauchery, every misdemeanour and questionable practice gleefully reported (and sometimes exaggerated) by spies who had infiltrated the English court.[17]

Francesco Giavarina observed in June 1656 that the defections to Charles from English ports were a big problem (but might have been bigger had Charles had access to a secure Continental port), with the result that an English Commonwealth fleet patrolled constantly in a line from Hull to Cadiz to intercept them.[18] How many failed to run this blockade is unknown. England was in turmoil. Giavarina observed that regular attempts were being made to discredit Charles by rumouring an invasion in force (not without good reason) and by circulating his intention to become a Catholic (unfounded, as will be seen, but a constant bugbear). The roads of England were full of soldiers marching east to the ports. Hull in particular was bursting with troops. Those who were known to have habitual royalist sympathies were imprisoned, their property seized. Torture for information became commonplace. There was even a plan to transport poorer royalists to Virginia. England had become a police state, suffering no dissent and led by a fearful if not paranoid government of regicides who now looked anxiously over their shoulders.[19]

It was not left to foreign spies alone to assess the dramatic effect of Charles's relative proximity. Writing to Sir Christopher Hatton III of Kirby Hall, Northamptonshire, Richard Lane, a royalist sympathiser (subsequently groom to Charles II's bedchamber) summed up the febrile atmosphere by the end of the summer when he wrote from Somerset House in London:

> 10 September 1656
> It is reported that Charles Stuart hath got a great army, which puts us in such a fright that we rest not night nor day. Great preparations are a making; the army is drawinge all to towne and recruitinge; the poore cavillers are by proclamation banishd the towne for six monthes; the ports are strictly guarded, and noe passes granted to goe out of the kingdome.[20]

Hatton himself, a staunch royalist, had been given special leave to return to England after years of exile, principally in Paris. He was, quite simply, flat broke. He was back at home within weeks of this letter being sent to him, his return passage presumably strictly monitored.

Against this background of uncertainty, the situation in Bruges quickly degenerated into one of ill-tempered edginess and distrust. In November 1656 it was reported that both the Flemish nobility and merchants in London were making their excuses and declining to trade or deal with Charles's court since they were so harried by English Commonwealth troops, ships and agents.[21] This was in some ways a replay of what happened after Edward IV had been in Bruges for a while. When trade suffered, Bruges took note!

Local traders had begun well disposed to the exiled Charles. They were advancing him money in considerable quantities to offset the absence of funds from the King of Spain but they too began to lose patience when the unpaid and increasingly unruly royalist troops began to despoil their shops, cargoes and livelihoods.[22] Giavarina noted late in 1657, and not by then without good reason, that the Flemings 'hate the English for their religion … and murder all that they get into their hands'. He may not have been exaggerating too much, although murders were probably few.[23]

Within the court, Charles did not help matters particularly. Around Christmas 1656 he and James, Duke of York, quarrelled and the duke left for Cologne via Holland. He was supported by their sister Mary, who was treated rudely as a result. James only returned in February 1657, during what became the bitterest winter and spring anyone had known for a generation, beset by heavy snow. It was so bad even the post failed to get through. Unable to do very much, even Charles's usual money-raising travels were short-lived.

Neither spring nor summer brought financial respite, not least since Charles was now re-organising his growing army into four brand-new regiments billeted in and around Bruges (including what would become the Grenadier Guards). Everyone was suffering. Charles's Secretary of State, Sir Edward Nicholas, wrote to his friend Sir Edward Hyde in April how he had bought a mourning suit for his late mother's anniversary but had had to make a cloak to go with it. Equally he had been unable to provide something similar for any of his family.[24]

Charles's own demeanour turned to pleasurable distractions as he despaired of any hope of being restored to his kingdom. There is no doubt he had the 'common touch', added to which he had already acquired a reputation as a ladies' man who was not easily dissuaded once his course was set. Some commentators, such as the Belgian Armand de Béhault de Dornan, have fought shy of confronting this, preferring a deferent view and noting 'the whole court's stay was one of wholly royal splendour'.[25] Not quite.

Not everyone close to Charles approved and a few were openly critical, suggesting he cultivate a little more mystique. In September 1657, Sir Edward Nicholas wrote from Bruges to his friend Hyde again, on the double problem of money and Charles's dalliances, which he linked as one:

> I am no less troubled at the inexcusable neglect of his Majesty than for his being disappointed of the money promised. But till the king shall himself take more majesty on him he will always and from all these peoples, find every day more and more neglect and disesteem, for they abhor the ridiculous freedom of the French, which makes no distinction of persons. I wish the king would set a better value on himself and not use familiarity with persons of so much inferior quality. But that is not to be said to him by any but yourself and those ... most in his confidence.[26]

The Earl of Ormonde, one of his closest confidantes, chided Charles, and it seemed to make a difference, but not for long. On one occasion Charles was so indiscreet during delicate negotiations that he had to be kneed hard from behind in a most un-deferential manner, simply to get him to shut up. In fact Cromwellian spies soon described the court as wholly debauched and amoral, not helped by Charles's lovesick attentions to (particularly) Catherine Pegge and Lucy Walter.

Charles had an affair with Catherine in 1657–8 and the relationship produced both a son and a daughter. She was generally compliant and kept a low profile but Lucy Walter became the archetypal woman scorned. Her relationship with Charles had ostensibly come to an end but she too had had a son by him, whose support and maintenance she sought with loud and ill-aimed abandon.[27] She hatched a plot to murder a royalist officer but the plan went wrong and he was only wounded. When the details got out and she was implicated, she threatened to publish her love letters from Charles if she was harmed and demanded more money in addition. She stayed in Brussels mostly but rattled Charles considerably, continuing to quarrel with royalist officers in the capital.

These were not the only ones, however. Payments at the time were made for the upkeep on Charles's behalf of a Netherlandish girl known as 'the infanta', her identity kept quiet, and a Frenchwoman called Janton, whom Charles called 'the best girl in the world'. Clearly the young Charles was giving characteristic vent to the sexual appetite of a man of twenty-seven but without any of the accompanying diplomacy or discretion required of his station.

Boredom and an apparent lack of hope combined to produce this situation, together with a natural deference to his advances among those whose paths he crossed. No doubt he was charming, but equally it was not easy to spurn the advances of a prince, however dispossessed he may have been. His closest companions were not immune either. In 1658 Princess Mary fell in love with a courtier and was censured by a Charles embroiled at the time with Lucy Walter. It was possibly a case of the pot calling the kettle black and Mary quickly lost her patience with her brother.

The money situation was no better as 1658 wore on. Sir Edward Nicholas noted in April in a letter to his friend Sir Harry Bennett,

> I can assure you that the king hath not yet received one Stuiver of the 6-months arrear due upon his ordinary allowance, and notwithstanding the 200,000 crowns sent to Don Juan [Prince Juan-José, the Spanish governor]. There was never any distressed king used with so much neglect as the King of England is here.[28]

Even the ever prolific Francesco Giavarina was aware that the king's hopes languished for lack of funds.[29] However, against such an impoverished royal backdrop it is perhaps surprising to note that payments were being made for the hire of tennis courts (games over which great sums were wagered), a tutor of Spanish and appearances by French comedians, harpists, and fiddlers. The tutor might be seen as a necessary engagement given the dealings with the Spanish court, but Charles was not known for his linguistic abilities although his French was fine. Previous Italian lessons had given rise to only a scurrilous and scatological love poem by the king, which he sent to a lover, and which ran, 'I am so in love with you that I cannot crap'; hardly the stuff of a great linguist.

Less explicable, when austerity was what was needed, are payments for his gambling losses in regular card games, the purchase of a pet monkey and a payment to a peddler who brought a camel to court for Charles's amusement. This was surely a court suffering from the depths of boredom, tired of its cultured surroundings and looking for the most hilarious, if not the basest distractions.

Charles's lack of regal dignity was widely noticed and he was lambasted for taking 'an immoderate delight in empty, effeminate and vulgar conversations', perhaps echoing the delicacy of his Italian love poetry.[30]

The indignity of the exiled king may have been a growing embarrassment. Far worse, however, was the increasingly ill-directed court as it went about its business in Bruges and elsewhere. Henry Proger, one of the equerries mentioned above, was implicated in the murder of a bona fide Commonwealth envoy while visiting the Spanish court in Madrid with Charles.[31] There were numerous petty squabbles in the backstreets, including some leading to duels. One dispute took place after the miscreants were caught urinating in the street of this industrious but conservative city. It is certain that such minor misdemeanours were common in every city of the period in the days before public conveniences, but the accusation was levelled because it was the English court at fault, and was probably fuelled by too much alcohol (both Bruges and Flanders have a long history of beer consumption). The poverty, squalor and unruly behaviour was too much for some, even English. In June 1658 Joseph Jane had had enough and wrote to John Nicholas that he was intending to quit the city, even (or perhaps especially) if his wife came to join him.[32]

All over Bruges and in the villages beyond were quartered increasingly unruly royalist troops, paid for from the Spanish purse but not controlled by anyone. Among them were English, Irish, and especially Scots, who scared the Flemings no end. Unable to get paid or fed properly, they pillaged and plundered the communities in which they were billeted. The result was predictable. The host city's defence of its foreign guests was weakened and French and Commonwealth spies passed easily among the disorderly lines. In all the uncertainty, prices went through the roof, not least where the exiles were concerned, since their credit was exhausted. Sir Edward Nicholas wrote to Joseph Jane, who does seem to have left Bruges at about that time:

Bruges, 15 July 1658
An alarum that the French gave us at the walles of the towne on satterday morning kept Don Juan here, having resolved to have followed the procession at Bruxelles, which he performed here at Bruges [possibly the Procession of the Holy Blood]. They took away some horses of my Lord Newburgh at the very gate, which could not come into the towne the evening before. Things must needes grow very deare in this place … The Duke of Gloucester is much

respected among the better sort here, although amongst the rabble the name of English is ungrateful to them.

Clearly the nervous secretary of state was wholly aware of the growing groundswell of resentment against their stay, although took care only to implicate 'the rabble'. The unruly English, Irish and Scots were largely undisciplined and represented a constant thorn in the authorities' side. However, in conservative, Catholic Flanders it was equally religious observance which could set tongues wagging and which perhaps presented the proverbial last straw which broke the camel's back. As has been seen Charles was not yet in Bruges when the first suggestions were put about that he was about to become a Catholic, music to the ears of his enemies in England.

The most unfortunate aspect of this rumour was not just that it kept resurfacing but that Charles could not quash it on any level, since for one his Catholic allies in Bruges, Brussels and Spain were all pleased to hear it and it helped draw them nearer to him, not least because they would gain great standing with Rome if they could reel in the English Crown, lost to the Holy Mother Church since the 1530s. Secondly Charles counted many Catholics among his loyal supporters at every level of the court, both among his own people and Bruges's society. Previous rumours concerning his brother James's intention to become a Catholic *were* true (although he would not formally convert until the 1660s). However, this one religious question continued to heap problems as the months went by. If he espoused Catholicism (or failed to distance himself sufficiently from it), he played into Cromwell's hands and lost support in England. But if he held out too strongly for his Protestant faith, he stood to alienate his hosts.[33] It was a balancing act he regularly had to make as the rumours just kept on resurfacing.

Soon after his arrival in Bruges, Charles had attended the provincial chapter of the English Carmelites, led of course by his supporter, the Prioress Lady Helen Bedingfield. That might have been as far as it went, and the decision might have been supportable, but he then went further and took part in a theological debate at the convent, risking accusations of having his Protestant faith perverted.[34]

Bruges today contains an English Protestant church, but in 1656–8 no such provision existed. It has been suggested that the basement of the Seven Towers was converted into a makeshift church for the court. Equally possible is the basement of the Casselberg.[35] The performance of the Protestant liturgy caused such consternation that the burgomaster and the bishop both voiced their opposition and demanded the city authorities take a hand in the matter. On 12 November 1657 the Council of Flanders ordered the magistrate to take all measures to put an end to the public liturgy of the 'Lutheran culte' and make a list of the entire English court's names.

The city magistrate felt unable to enforce such sanctions and on 27 November he wrote to the Governor General, Prince Juan-José, who instead stated that it more concerned the King of Spain himself, probably because Charles and his court were the king's guests. Nevertheless the governor did respond a month later and stated that the Council of Flanders ought to observe the laws concerning the defence of the right to practise the Protestant faith at Bruges, but that it could not tolerate this religion being practised in the hotel of the King of England, for his person, his servants and domestics.[36] This suggests that the tradition of the cellars becoming a makeshift church is true either up to this point or thereafter. Certainly afterwards it seems that the Anglican Communion had to be held in secret.[37] Later on in 1659 Charles sought to provide for Anglicans whose relatives had died at court, and who served and died at Bruges, by having set aside a piece of land for a separate cemetery for Protestants. It seems to have been short-lived and no longer exists.

In the end Charles himself was forced to write an extraordinary letter to the minister of the English church at Amsterdam to set out his position. Writing from Brussels on 7 November 1658 he stated that

> the world cannot but take notice of Our constant and uninterrupted profession and exercise of it in those places where the contrary Religion is only practised and allowed [thereby perhaps admitting the clandestine services in Bruges] ... we value Our selfe soe much upon that part of Our title of being Defender of the Faith that noe worldly temptations can ever prevayle with Us to swarve from it and the Protestant Religion in which We have been bredd, the propagation whereof We shall endeavour with Our utmost power.[38]

Charles himself left Bruges in early 1658 for Dunkirk and military operations, perhaps moved on as much as anything by another bitter winter that left the exiles writing longingly for their homeland. Although most of his court remained in Bruges in cultured if chilly surroundings, their appreciation of their hosts, as has been seen, did not run deep. Charles returned for a while in the spring of 1659 but was then granted a home in Brussels, which he shared with his brothers between March and August of that year. His eventual departure from there seems to have been brought about by political intrigue and espionage from England.

The still febrile situation can be gauged from a letter from Sir Edward Nicholas to Charles Siledon (an assumed name for a royalist Mr Johnson):

> Sir, in obedience to your commands I have ventured this by the post of Flanders, but I shall humbly beg to be excused for the future, the merchants assuring me that their letters as well as to as from thence, are frequently

opened and examined, and anything in cipher will so disturb Thurlow that, although he decipher it not, he will not be quiet till he have traced it to the person.[39]

The lengths to which the royalists had to go with their diplomatic post was considerable. One noted to Sir Edward Nicholas that same month that

> there hath been noe post either by way of Antwerp or France. Upon Monday was 14 dayes I writ by way of Paris, as you directed, and upon Thursday last by way of Rouen to be sent to … Antwerp as Lord Chancellor commanded me, and lastly I writ to Lord Chancellor by ship to Rotterdam.[40]

These were convoluted postal routes indeed. Direct communication seems to have become impossible.

Charles, in order to sidestep the intrigue, moved away to Hoogstraeten, near the frontier, and travelled to Antwerp, Breda and The Hague. However, here there were insufficient lodgings for the court, who remained at Bruges. Charles travelled about with six or so companions, at last relatively incognito.[41] In late May he attended a sumptuous party given in his honour at Bernay near Paris, with his mother, the widowed queen. This was a noteworthy 'treatment' (as it was termed) and went on from mid-afternoon until dawn the following day. It began with music indoors, followed by a play in the garden, a farce, and then 'an extraordinarie supper with great disorder'. After this they were treated to a ballet of seven acts, fireworks on the water and two hours of dancing, all rounded off by a breakfast banquet until dawn.[42]

By mid-1659 the political situation in England began to change and with the sudden death of Oliver Cromwell and the brief and inept rule of his son Richard, Charles felt safe enough to return to Brussels.

From there on 1 August he went in secret to Calais, Boulogne, and onward in a diplomatic tour via La Rochelle and Toulouse to Saragossa and Fuentarabia in Spain. There Lord Culpepper wrote that 'the king is in perfect good health and hath strangely wonn upon the affection of all here'.[43] Strangely won indeed, given the salacious stories which must have preceded him, not least to ultraconservative Spain. Clearly he had not lost his charm but here in Spain he did not linger long enough for the novelty to wear off.

By the end of 1659 Charles had returned to Brussels. However, he did not venture back to Bruges. He was only a few months away from the restoration of the English monarchy.

9

ORDINARY LIVES, EXTRAORDINARILY LIVED

This book has covered selected royal experiences through the entire medieval period and the privileged of a number of countries, principally England with Wales, Scotland and France, many of whom were related to each other. Their exiles were spread right across Europe. What is clear is that, taking in such a length of time and such a geographical spread of exiles, hostages, prisoners and their 'hosts' necessarily involves a wide range of personalities, for whom the prospect of a stretch in prison, a period as a hostage (whether with a prospect of ransom or not) or a period of exile, ranging from a few months to a lifetime's banishment, held a wide variety of fears and concerns. Such concerns were trivial to some, whose records seem to make light of them, but were insurmountable to others.

In conclusion, a broader look at the circumstances of an exile or captivity adds both complementary detail and also contrast and the distinctiveness of individual experiences. The detail clearly could have devastating effects on an individual, for whom the prospect of a very long stretch, or that of banishment beyond the bounds of Christendom, felt like (and could be) a barely disguised death sentence.

Character was clearly at play in the way individuals took their peculiar circumstances and merely attempted to survive them or managed to draw on reserves of inner strength and endless patience to thrive. Of Henry Tudor, Jasper Tudor said on meeting the youth, 'This trewly, this is he unto whom both we and our adversaryes must yeald and geave over the domynion.'[1] Since his formative years had already been marked by life as a near permanent hostage at Raglan Castle, the immediate move to Brittany, with its linguistic and perceived cultural Celtic bonds with Wales, may not have been overly worrying, although he cannot have been helped by a prolonged spell in the daunting keep of Largoët, stultifying in its isolation and even today marked by a morose stillness which is almost tangible. For Henry Tudor, however, it was the brief handover back to an English embassy which unbalanced him, resulting in his nerve giving way temporarily. He clearly came to see his continued exile as his key to safety and a measured return to England; any circumstances not controlled by him represented certain death. He may have been right.

Single-mindedness and common courtesy were key to those who felt they had little to lose but everything to gain. Edward IV knew what he needed to do in order to end his own exile and made plans quickly and thoroughly, taking care to foster the best relations with his gracious hosts who already knew and trusted him from the sumptuous wedding celebrations of his sister to the Duke of Burgundy two years previously.

Of Edward IV, William Habington said, 'Certainly never liv'd prince whom adversitie did more harden into action; and prosperitie more often to voluptuousnesse.'[2] Despite arriving in Flanders with nothing but the clothes on their backs and hardly a penny to their name, he and his court were pitched headlong into the civic life of Bruges as if they had lived there all along. Entertained and genuinely welcomed, they were able to partake fully of what their temporary home had to offer and although their ultimate host, the Duke of Burgundy, eventually felt (and indeed was) compromised by the arrangement and said as much, this was power politics on a grand scale beginning to weigh in the balance. No one can doubt, however, that heartfelt hospitality on the ground was never in short supply. The exiled court reciprocated by ensuring its popularity made for a grand send-off when the time came to leave. Bruges had already shown its capacity for unstinting hospitality to the Duke of Orleans on his eventual release from England in 1440, and the wedding party to end them all for the marriage of Charles the Bold and Margaret of York in 1468. Edward's brother, the young Richard of Gloucester, had already spent a short while there as a child in exile earlier in the Wars of the Roses and had been well cared for. Perhaps Edward knew he was in for a good time at Bruges, however long he might stay, fêted with a hospitality which would lighten the worst boredom and make light of the direst predictions of doom. Bruges remains the most hospitable of cities today.

That prosperity led to excess, as Habington relates of Edward (writing for a seventeenth-century, partly Puritan audience), may have been true across the broad sweep of his entire reign. Perhaps overall it was, and commentators agree, marked by some considerable perjury and periods of debauchery and sexual abandon.[3] However, there is no evidence that such excess marked any of his time in Flanders and the extent to which, as an unintended ambassador for England without his crown, he endeared himself to the people of Bruges was testament to a period of cultured discretion and gracious acceptance of his lot. His presence may have become awkward for his brother-in-law, the Duke of Burgundy, hastening his return, but he was certainly not, as Habington described him, 'a miserable exile'.[4] It is ironic that Habington was writing only a few years before the incarceration of his own monarch, Charles I, and the exile of the Prince of Wales, later Charles II. Neither was generally miserable, though they had cause to be. Both believed in themselves and their cause, and both took their pleasure where they found it, if to differing degrees.

It was perhaps for a writer such as Habington the idea of the physical state of separation from hearth, home and kin which instilled fear, scared by Biblical stories of the wanderings and exile of Israel. For a medieval monarch, entirely used to life on the move and a dozen different homes and castles, travel, however distant, held few fears.

The avoidance of death in the face of total defeat did not mean that capture, imprisonment and ransom were inevitable. In the early thirteenth century William Longsword, Earl of Salisbury, proved that. In 1225 he was returning from Gascony where he had been on the king's business.[5] On the journey he was shipwrecked on the Ile de Ré where he was forced into hiding at a period in which western Aquitaine was going through one of its periodic pro-French (or at least anti-English) periods. The guard was out across enemy territory and spies were everywhere, searching for the dashing earl in what became a classic escape and evasion of its day. He is said to have been betrayed a number of times but on each occasion escaped in the nick of time; he spent some time in a monastery and just as much time moving about in disguise on a journey which took him many months to get home. As befits such an odyssey, his ravishing wife, Countess Ela, the noted society beauty of her day, was reputedly being courted by an unscrupulous noble suitor who quickly gave the earl up for dead and made for his available 'widow' with unseemly haste. For whatever reason (and that part may be a later story to enhance their own subsequent reputations) she resisted, and was reunited with William on his return amid tales of his six months on the run behind enemy lines.

Disguise was a common theme throughout the period. Henry Tudor (Henry VII), Charles I and Richard the Lionheart all adopted disguises at one time or another, with varying degrees of success. In an age where recognisable likenesses were few and far between, good descriptions circulated and the bearing of a monarch or noble might be enough to give away the uncomfortable fit of a ragged set of unseemly clothes. Otherwise, disguises were commonly adopted by any who wished to gain access to an exile or prisoner, such as the messenger who dressed as a fisherman to gain access to the captive Charles I returning from an afternoon's bowling.

Similarly Gustav Ericsson, a noble of the Swedish house of Vasa, having been taken as a hostage by King Christian of Denmark, escaped from his prison on the island of Jutland in September 1519 dressed as a cowherd.[6]

His flight was first to Lübeck, lead city of the then anti-Danish Hanseatic League, where he met mutual allies against Denmark, and then on to his native Sweden by unassuming fishing boat, where he began to raise a peasants' rebellion against the oppressor. Edward IV too escaped by fishing boat, unable to board a more obvious vessel fit for a king. Richard the Lionheart also had to change boats to give pursuers the slip. In such cases the boat owners took considerable risk to their lives and livelihood to ferry the erstwhile captives and exiles.

Not all nobles could act according to gallant and chivalric codes when the test came. Fear of what terrible fate awaited them drove some men to a breakdown. For his part in a plot against Richard II, and perhaps fearing that he would share the fate of the Duke of Gloucester (suffocated seemingly on the king's order), in 1397 the otherwise redoubtable and cultured Thomas Beauchamp, Earl of Warwick, burst into tears at court before throwing himself on the king's mercy awaiting the royal decision. He was banished to the Isle of Man where he was to spend the rest of Richard's days imprisoned.[7] Although the banishments of Richard II's last parliaments were reversed by Henry IV in 1399, Thomas was never the same man and died in 1401.

Some, like Faulkes de Bréauté in 1224, were utterly broken by their experiences. Faulkes, an Anglo-Norman action man whose nickname had become 'the rod of the Lord's fury' from his fearsome battle prowess, became caught up in power struggles under the boy king Henry III. His family loyalties sucked him into his rebellious brother William's stand against the king at Bedford Castle and as a result he was banished, having had to attend the king under safe conduct passes twice in three months, stretching the meaning of the word 'allegiance'. His brother was executed. Although Faulkes himself was never present at Bedford, his complicity was beyond question, although he retained friends in high places. His lands were forfeit, his goods sold and he was banished, harshly, as some contemporaries felt. He was said to be a broken man and lasted barely two years.[8]

The story of Thomas Mowbray, Duke of Norfolk, is similar. Although he had once been a childhood friend of his king, Richard II, Mowbray was banished for life by him in 1398 after an infamous tournament, nominally to the death, at Coventry opposite Henry of Bolingbroke, the future Henry IV. With the contest sensationally halted by the king before any blood was shed, his sentence was specifically to 'quit the realm for the rest of his life, and ... choose whether he would dwell in Prussia, in Bohemia or in Hungary or would go right beyond the sea to the land of Saracens and unbelievers'.[9] Many at the time thought the punishment harsh.

One of the last mentions that Mowbray merits is in his successful application in February 1399 to the Senate of Venice for the loan of a galley to take him to Jerusalem on pilgrimage. Ironically it was backed up by letters of commendation from the same Richard II who had only just banished him forever. Having made his pilgrimage he returned to Venice but was overcome by plague shortly after, his condition probably not helped by the news that his bereft wife, the duchess, had died soon after his departure. The debt he owed his ship's captain for his pilgrimage remained unpaid when he died and restitution was still being sought from his heirs in 1408.[10] His body was buried in Venice where it was eventually forgotten until his memorial stone was sought out and returned by a later Duke of Norfolk in the nineteenth century.

By contrast, Mowbray's fellow protagonist, Henry Bolingbroke, was banished for ten years, with no such stipulation over the distance to be put between him and England. His sentence was later reduced to six years. A cultured and exceptionally well-travelled man already, he ended up at the French court in Paris, where he was royally entertained and thoroughly enjoyed himself until his hosts realised that he was an enemy of the English state, which further strained an already difficult cross-Channel relationship. His eventual departure from Paris was the start of his return to England to claim the throne as Henry IV.

While Bolingbroke made the most of his travelling opportunity, the highest status was no bar to suggestions of a steep physical and mental decline or a sudden, sticky end. Witness Henry VI's brief second confinement in the Tower of London in 1471, or indeed Richard II's own swift end, being said to have starved himself to death in Pontefract Castle, a well-known prison stronghold. No one can forget the silent end to the lives of the young princes in the Tower of London in 1483, whatever the exact circumstances of their still controversial demise. Their untimely end has forever since helped define the short reign of Richard III, once an exile in Bruges alongside his older brother Edward IV, as one of brutality.

Previously in 1202, King John had seemingly connived in having the young Arthur of Brittany, principal Anglo-Breton claimant to that duchy – and his own nephew – murdered while in his captivity in Normandy, an act for which he was universally condemned by his contemporaries, despite a paucity of good evidence. It perhaps did not help his cause that the boy's body was reportedly dumped in the River Seine. In every case, however, even the occasionally lax mores of the day had been overstepped and condemnation was swift and unforgiving.

In some cases a lifetime's incarceration, despite being cocooned and relatively well looked after as a hostage, meant that little or no telling of their story whatsoever, whether partisan or independent, ever emerged. They are simply never on stage to live a life which might draw comment. Thus the hapless Eleanor of Brittany, sister of the murdered Arthur, is first recorded as being a ward of the English royal court in 1189. After a period of freedom, she was taken prisoner in 1196 at fifteen by her estranged stepfather Ranulf, 6th Earl of Chester. They were caught up between Richard the Lionheart and Philip Augustus of France in a titanic battle for the soul of Brittany and the duchy's leanings towards either England or France. Eleanor watched her mother contract leprosy while a captive alongside her at St James-de-Beuvron (Manche, France), was handed to the English Crown, was helpless when her mother died and her brother Arthur was murdered, and then lived out all her days in a succession of castles, chiefly Corfe, until her death in 1241, aged sixty. For much of that time she had been kept under strict guard 'under the kepyng of foure men, that there shuld be no frute of her wombe'.[11] It was intended that the very valid family claim she held to the Duchy of Brittany would never be allowed to flourish or spread to another generation. This cynical policy probably meant that once her childbearing years had passed by in barren isolation she became a rather sorry figure of the old maid at the head of an irrelevant court in exile, whose only experience of the world outside was shrouded in childhood memory of an age gone by. Her own silence in the record is deafening, apart from occasional castle purchases for her diet. Saddest of all, her jailers were all members of her family, Ranulf her stepfather; Richard and John, both uncles; and Henry III, her first cousin.

Being locked up was not the end for some who had friends in high places. Sometimes negotiations could be relatively swift, if low-key, to effect a release, occasionally against the odds. The scheming of others seems to make a mockery of their situation; perhaps that was their intention.

The almost piratical King Charles of Navarre, aptly named 'Charles the Wicked', was sprung from jail in 1357, in Wild West fashion, despite being widely acknowledged as a thoroughly nasty piece of work. Charles, more recently described as 'talented, enterprising, but treacherous', had been arrested at Rouen in April 1356 for the murder of the Constable of France.[12] For this he had been imprisoned by the French king, Jean II, at a castle near Amiens. From there, however, he was in regular contact with his relative the dowager Queen Isabella, mother to Edward III. She ensured that regular news was brought to her of Charles while every effort was made for his release, diplomacy complicated by the Battle of Poitiers, after which of course Jean II himself became a hostage of France. In the same November of 1357 that Isabella entertained the French hostages of Poitiers, she received the news that she had waited for, that Charles had been sprung from his prison by his countrymen. That they were in England's pay is not in doubt. The newly freed Charles marched on Paris straightaway, took it and held it for England against the Dauphin, shattering hopes of an early peace settlement between England and France.[13] His own close shave seems to have made little difference to his actions. He barely broke step.

Some exiles, holding out little hope of a restoration to their former lives, made the most of their new one and tried to have one long party, sometimes leading to a surfeit and endless boredom, as was the case with England's Charles II, whose tumultuous court was eventually a major part of his outstaying his welcome among his otherwise generous hosts in Bruges. The persistent difficulties that Charles's Protestant Christian faith caused in fervently Catholic Bruges, hot on the heels of its own painful religious wars, might have been a proving ground for two otherwise sensible and confident courts, but for the repeated stupidity of a small number of individuals (probably including Charles) whose irresponsible actions brought the exiles into disrepute in what had become a reserved and conservative environment. The hosts' faith was certainly affronted but so was their official cultural dignity. The exiles, guests or not, just became too embarrassing, so openly did some flout the mores of the day.

For others the length of their captivity probably weighed very heavily indeed. While little is known of the effects that a lifetime as a hostage had on Eleanor of Brittany, the twenty-five years as a hostage in England spent by Charles, Duke of Orleans, brought increasing pain as he noted with anguish the successive deaths of his second (and beloved) wife and only daughter far off. His lament that he felt utterly alone at the time was probably not far from the truth. For quite some time even his political role as pawn trying to soften Anglo–French relations paled into relative insignificance for the period that the two countries were undeniably at loggerheads. It did not serve Charles well that on his deathbed Henry V expressly wished Orleans's imprisonment to continue, at least until Henry VI came of age. Even then the Duke of Gloucester and those who supported the strongest resistance to French peace overtures wanted Charles kept secure, despite the majority recognising his diminished potential role with the passage of time. It took the personal intervention of an enlightened young Henry VI and the influence of the Duke of Burgundy to bring about Charles's release. Ironically, once back in his duchy he married for a third time and sired the next King of France, Louis XII; unsurprisingly, Louis was anti-England by default.

The laments of a stranded family at home are seldom mentioned. Charles's wife and daughter are the ones missed, yet they too must have missed him. So too when Jean de Joinville went off to the Sixth Crusade in 1249, he tells of his own sorrow at passing his home on the banks of the Rhone as he sailed. There is scant mention of his family's feelings for him, knowing that the journey of a crusader was one of the most hazardous any man could undertake. Their probable fears were almost realised when he was taken prisoner and cruelly treated, almost dying in Egypt, at the hands of the sultan. Had he done so, as likely as not they would never have found out what happened to him. They would simply have the memory of his passing by in a boat heading for the sea.

Age

Age was no barrier to the greatest pressures being applied in order to oust, remove or disbar someone from their claims to power or to remove them from 'harm's way', seeking their safety in a pointedly euphemistic and wholly hurtful move, as can be seen in the case of, for instance, the young Henry Tudor, forced out by a renascent Edward IV, and perhaps most pointedly his contemporaries, the ill-fated Princes in the Tower.

Among the youngest exiles was perhaps David II, King of Scotland. Born in 1324, he was only five years old when he came to the throne, was 'married' and was deposed by the time he was eleven. Defeated by the English at the Battle of Halidon Hill in 1333 he fled within a year to a welcoming France which saw its chances to ally itself with him and his advisors against England, which meanwhile had advanced its own (very valid) claimant to the Scots throne, Edward Balliol, who, at the head of an English army (never welcome!), was crowned in opposition. Scotland now had two crowned heads of state. The young David was fêted by the French king, Philip VI, who settled him and his equally young queen in Château Gaillard, high above the River Seine. Here he was 'safe', within reach of the French court at Paris as befitted an ally and confidant and only a stone's throw from England, a nose royally thumbed at the English throne, which had built that magnificent stronghold in the 1190s and lost it to France so spectacularly in a six-month siege of 1203–4. Memories were long and France and England were again at loggerheads.

Rival claims and matters in Scotland were sufficiently changed for David to return home in 1341 and begin again to govern in Scotland, still only a young man of seventeen. However, history was to repeat itself within a short time as David was rash enough to invade England and was thoroughly beaten and himself captured at the Battle of Neville's Cross (County Durham) in 1346. He was taken initially to London and then to Windsor, but soon transferred to Odiham Castle in Hampshire, an old stronghold built by John in the early thirteenth century. There he was kept for eleven years, almost as far south of Scotland as it was possible to be, until the promise of payment of a ransom of 100,000 marks and the withdrawal of Edward Balliol's claims to the Scots throne brought his release by a more conciliatory Edward III, now sure of Scotland's ineffectual part in his ongoing struggles with France.

Throughout the episode Balliol had been largely supported by grants from the English exchequer, from which, long after his royal claim was null and void, he still claimed large sums of English cash, ceding his own Continental property in Ponthieu in the end to secure English finances in his dotage.[14]

David's captivity was contemporary for a time with that of the French king, Jean II. These were golden years for Edward III, whose power over his neighbours was thus without parallel. For 1356–7 the giddy feeling of having two neighbouring kings captive must have been intoxicating and the English power engendered by Jean's incarceration almost certainly helped facilitate David's release.

The choice of residence for a hostage taken in battle depended to some extent upon their status and the favour and esteem in which they were held. Naturally a king or queen would involve the greatest amount of thought and preparation as to the venue for their stay. They needed to be allowed something like a retinue which reflected their station and, in time, they would need quarters suitable for the reception and entertainment of visitors, as well as the inevitable party of armed guards who would shadow their every movement, looking after their 'safety and security' as the terminology went.

This thinking is behind the choice of accommodation for Jean II of first the Savoy Palace, called 'the fairest manor in England', when times were good and later, in more difficult times, the castle of Somerton in Lincolnshire amid a flat, almost featureless landscape and big sky. Berkhamsted castle was actually little more than a short stopover, so widespread conversion to King Jean's use was probably not a priority. Few places had the space and connections suitable to support a royal court. There was more to it than this, however, and Somerton and Berkhamsted both had, or acquired, a pedigree as places of confinement. They were clearly both suitable in the short term, if a little dour, as was Hertford, where the dowager Queen Isabella had held an elegant court. The Duke of Bourbon was imprisoned for a few months at Somerton in the early fifteenth century, having been captured at Agincourt in 1415; he was moved there from Portchester, on his way to Pontefract Castle. Meanwhile Somerton had also been the prison of Margaret de Manny, widow of Sir Walter de Manny, a famous knight of his generation and founder of the London Charterhouse. Her guards were to 'lead her as quietly and honourably as they can ... to Somerton ... the king wills that she shall stay there for some time, and to deliver her to the constable thereof'.[15] She was presumably there when Queen Isabella visited and her own needs were presumably better suited to a castle which had a female overlord.

At Berkhamsted, one poor prisoner may have got caught up in the frenetic activity around the French king's brief imprisonment there. One John Driver, described as 'a felon', was taken on 5 June 1359 and held in the king's prison there, where he died only a few days later (whether due to poor conditions or injuries is not mentioned). The coroner's inquest was carried out within days.[16]

It is not always easy to know why royal hostages were moved when they were, unless during periods of national alarm (when a necessary move might take place with little notice). The move was not always away from the source of apparent danger, however. Thus when King Jean II was moved from Somerton Castle on 20 March 1360, amid French raiding, it was south – towards the origin of unrest, the South Coast, if only briefly, before going to the Tower where he would be most secure in the run-up to his release. As ransom negotiations became more delicate, so the need to ensure no deal-busting jailbreak was possible became paramount.

For those of lesser rank the choice of prison was relatively wide, and depended upon the degree of trust which could be placed in the hostage; they were, after all, on parole. A number of favourites can be seen throughout the medieval period, a hierarchy topped by the Tower of London, where any number of prisoners of different rank and nationality can be found year on year. Others emerged, such as Pontefract Castle and Pevensey Castle, although neither was a permanent residence for someone of exceptional rank. It was simply that there was usually a good garrison there to 'protect' the prisoners. After Agincourt, Pontefract Castle acquired new kitchen and brewhouse ranges, probably because of the large numbers of high-ranking hostages lodged there with their courts for months on end.

Caernarfon and Conwy Castles were major prisons in the years following Agincourt in 1415 under both Henry V and his infant son Henry VI. North Wales was as far from France as could be imagined, both geographically and culturally, and a Welsh kinship with Breton culture, itself problematic for the French, would cause them some discomfort if they plotted an escape. A group of twelve noble prisoners were taken to Conwy in 1422 by Sir John Bolde, where they were set for an unspecified stay before being taken to the Tower, presumably for ease of ransom and release.[17] Other castles in the area, such as Rhuddlan, were also used as prisons after the Agincourt and Harfleur campaigns.

The Tower of London too held any number of captive knights. After the Battle of Harfleur, Henry V was making arrangements for a group of seventeen French barons and knights, all in the Tower, hostages taken by James, King of Scotland. Together their immediate keep cost the English king over £314.[18]

At times there were trustworthy prisoners and hostages (whose parole was unlikely to be broken) all over the country. Many may not have been under especial guard, some perhaps lodged in monastic guest houses or the homes of minor gentry whose expenses simply do not show up in national registers. Visits to cathedrals and abbeys were not uncommon, since the Church was universal, did not (at least overtly) usually take sides and could be relied upon for fitting hospitality. In this way Jean II was a guest of both Lincoln's and St Albans's cathedral abbeys. Such a diaspora of prisoners was not conducive to easy administration, however. Thus in 1370, Walter de la Roke was sent by the king to treat with the remaining French hostages of the Poitiers campaigns and their aftermath. De la Roke had to travel to Warwickshire, Leicestershire, Nottinghamshire, Derbyshire, Lichfield and Coventry to do his business as they were still spread far and wide. Unsurprisingly the greatest expense on his account was hire of horses.[19]

For the highest-ranking captives and hostages, it was as much the choice of host that might exercise the king and his counsel as to the venue. It was necessary to ensure that neither the captive nor the host was embarrassed or inconvenienced by the new and unexpected arrival. While the captive had no power to decide anything, the host could rarely refuse the king. The king naturally did not wish to make unpopular choices that would bring resentment, easily done if the captive came with a court of twenty, along with thirty or more retainers (grooms, cooks, pastry-chefs, a butler and a cellarer), baggage and horses. The list is immense.

Thus getting the choice of host and venue right was key. For such as the Duke of Orleans, such choices were needed time and again over a quarter of a century, for he was a cultured man who was used to great wealth and a sensitive reception. He for one was exceedingly well treated and, despite the obvious privations which emanate from standing helpless when his wife and daughter died, was subsequently stable and contented enough with his lot to allow himself to fall in love and pursue a young lady, if only for a short while. His hosts for the most part were cultured men, with whom he shared interests and outlooks.

Fitting In

It was one thing to have an exile, hostage or prisoner foisted upon one's household, but quite another to be that person and have to fit in. Not to do so was a problem for the criticism it attracted for both guest and host.

The late medieval noble household was intended to be a reflection of God's heaven, with strict hierarchies, etiquette and protocols to be observed. The introduction of a separate and segregated person of rank, sometimes with their own household of retainers, put incredible pressure upon the rank and file who made daily provision for their own masters. There might be differences in language, mores and customs and then there was the simple fact that two masters, of potentially different rank, rubbed shoulders in one house. It was a recipe for trouble. Little wonder that so many hosts petitioned the Crown to be relieved of the burden and that the Crown often sought to ring the changes after a while. William Cecil, Lord Burghley, while responsible for managing the Earl of Shrewsbury's very costly wardship of Mary, Queen of Scots, at the same time advised his own son regarding hospitality to 'let thy hospitality be moderate and according to the measure of thine own estate, rather plentiful than sparing – but not too costly – for I never knew any grow poor by keeping an orderly table'.[20]

If it might seem to modern eyes that a foreign exchange student was living in for a while, add to that a degree of high social status, a diet befitting such a rank, a need for amusement to prevent boredom and a body of retainers, with horses and a need for victuals who might outnumber one's own staff and livery, and the scale of the challenge for a chosen host becomes clearer. There was the capacity for a poor choice of host to result in that household being bankrupted, fractured and just plain inconvenienced beyond all measure. The Earl of Shrewsbury, hosting Mary, Queen of Scots, is a case in point. That he genuinely grew very close to her was a real problem. Her alleged affection for him, which may or may not have been deep-seated, but certainly made the countess jealous, might be seen in some eyes as an example of Stockholm syndrome. The rumour of a love child had its roots in discrediting Mary, but the earl and countess were severely discomfited. There may have been little in it since the countess was well known for her rage, eventually occasioning a note from the Bishop of Lichfield who admitted to the earl in 1590 (when the earl was considering separation) that she was 'a sharp and bitter shrew, and therefore like enough to shorten your life, if she would keep you company'.[21]

Unforeseen complications were a particular problem. Quarrels and fights among guest-courts were not unknown. While a case of wounding in the court of Jean II at Hertford was dealt with internally, the constant excesses of the young Prince Charles in Bruges were an embarrassment to his court, which sought constantly to keep a lid on his wayward leanings. Surrounded by a ragtag royalist army, daily growing too numerous to be quartered sensibly and often unpaid for lengths of time by the cash-strapped court in exile, their raucous and drunken behaviour became the gossip and bugbear of Flanders.

Charles, Duke of Orleans, was moved on one occasion to prevent his love affair becoming an embarrassment, not to him but to his hosts, while Mary, Queen of Scots has been linked romantically to her jailer, the Earl of Shrewsbury (although scurrilous rumour aided her detractors immensely). While his personal heartbreak at her execution and his wife's jealousy of Mary, whose estate can hardly have been the stuff of envy, indicate a real attachment on the one hand and a perceived one on the other, such an attachment was doomed from the start.

Love, and more particularly lust, was potentially a problem. For the libidinous young Prince Charles in Bruges in the 1650s, his persistent conduct was an embarrassment to his court and the lengthening list of his conquests was to become a hallmark of his colourful life. Some of his courtesans resented him, while others happily basked in the glow of his charisma and later the knowledge of continuing to have the king's ear as well as the rest of him.

The Welsh Henry Tudor is said to have acquired a Breton lover in the 1470s, probably while he was in Vannes, but nothing is known of her, not even her name, except perhaps that she was the mother of his illegitimate son, who was later appointed constable of Beaumaris Castle on Anglesey in another recognition of the bonds between the Welsh and Breton cultures. It is unproven but intriguing that, had the two married, that child, rather than going to Anglesey, would have enjoyed precedence over any Prince Arthur or Henry (Henry VIII).

Just occasionally an enforced stay in a foreign land is encountered that ought to be pleasant but isn't. A sojourn which does not qualify as an exile, but in the minds of the interested parties probably felt like one, occurred in 1506 to King Philip of Castile and his queen, Juana,[22] whose winter journey with their court from the Low Countries to Spain was to become a nightmare. The story is related by a Venetian diplomat in England, Ambassador Quirini, who described the queen as follows, with no diplomacy at all: 'She was mad, miserly and jealous, and does not allow women in her court' (which was a consequence of being suspicious of her husband and paranoid about philandering, whether real or imagined).[23]

The king and queen embarked at Armuiden on 7 January but adverse winds kept them in port for three days; when they finally got under way their fleet ran headlong into a storm off Southampton, which drove them into the Bay of Biscay. Although on 13 January they enjoyed a calm sea it was too brief and the following day a gale-force west-sou'wester drove them full onto the English South Coast. Four ships made Plymouth, three Dartmouth and three others foundered on rocks. A worse January had not been seen in living memory.

With the Plymouth contingent was the Venetian ambassador to England, whose finer sensibilities were wholly affronted by his encounter with Cornwall and the uncouth, unintelligible (in his view) Cornish whose language he was unable to speak. His complaints were unceasing and he was stuck in Falmouth and Plymouth for weeks on end while his ship was repaired.

The king was almost killed. His ship actually capsized but was then righted, when the sodden sails and cables were cut away. They were then able to put in. Both their status and their relationship by marriage to the English royal house guaranteed that Henry VII received them warmly and King Philip was entertained at Richmond while his ship was repaired at Falmouth. Queen Juana, meanwhile, her marriage being very shaky indeed, was allowed to go separately to Romford in Essex where she stayed for two months. She was widely considered to be unstable and her distance was for everyone's sake.

Once repairs were complete, Henry VII took what must have been a strained farewell of his estranged guests and they made separately for Falmouth to rejoin their own still disgruntled Venetian guest. For a while Philip got no further than Reading as he was ill. The queen, travelling in a manner unbecoming a lady, had got only as far as Exeter and stopped. When both resumed they finally reassembled at Falmouth on 30 March. Here they were forced, by bad weather, to stay for another month despite attempts to put out. It was a difficult stay as they were now thrown together by circumstances. They were poorly provisioned (in royal terms) and the distance from London meant that luxuries came overland at a very high price indeed. They were relieved to set sail on 23 April, arriving in Corunna three days later, the warring partners presumably glad to get out once more from under each other's feet.

The Cost of Upkeep

In England exiles, captives and hostages were maintained at the cost of the Crown until 1424.

Some individuals were costly from the outset. Exiled to the Isle of Man by Richard II, the Earl of Warwick cost over £1,000 for his upkeep, his Manx home being unable to foot his bill.[24] Strange perhaps then that the experience broke the earl, unless he did not see the fruits of his jailer's largesse, paid as it was to an intermediary, in this case the Earl of Wiltshire and Treasurer of England. It is always an unanswered question as to how much of the expenses claims was real or fraudulent. Little changes it seems.

Such costs soared on occasions and the change of 1424 was brought about by the sheer numbers incarcerated after rebellion in Wales and seemingly endless wars in France and Brittany.

The years after Agincourt and Harfleur saw repeated payments from the exchequer for large numbers of the French nobility, held in England and sent off to a dozen castles across the realm to kick their heels and await hostage-bargaining (a sell-off between interested parties) and hopefully ransom. The twenty-five-year incarceration of the Duke of Orleans was not typical of his fellow captives of Agincourt. Throughout the period 1415–24 records are strewn with entries of expense payments to castle constables for the groups of French prisoners they were charged with keeping: seventeen in the Tower of London; twenty-four at Nottingham; twelve at Conwy; twenty at Caernarfon, twenty at Rhuddlan and two at Calais.[25]

During Edward III's reign the going rate for the upkeep of a single knight seems to have been 2 shillings a day, but the expenses of a ducal household could be enormous. Edward paid 40s a day for the household of the relatively minor Edward Balliol, his claimant to the Scots throne. This increased in wartime to 60s per day.[26] A middle-ranking noble, whether English or foreign, under Henry VI might cost £1 6s 8d a week for his or her upkeep.[27]

When a prominent captive became ill, no one wanted the spotlight to fall on them and what rudimentary medicine was available was quickly administered. The experience of Mary, Queen of Scots was certainly not typical, although her condition may not have been brought to everyone's attention for fear of the opprobrium it would attract. When David Bruce, hostage King of Scotland, fell sick at Odiham Castle in Hampshire, payments for an apothecary and the components of his medicine added 25 per cent to the cost of his upkeep. His sickness may have reflected a relative meanness shown to him by the English Crown. For a while both he and Edward Balliol were Edward III's guests. Balliol was drawing 40s per day, David Bruce a mere 13s 4d (1 mark) a day. When the Crown bought new clothes for David in July 1357, they comprised a jacket, a tunic, a pair of stockings, three pairs of socks, cloth for a robe and its lining, a hat ribbon and two pairs of linen cloths, totalling £5 6s 2d. It was hardly the stuff of royalty. In August of the same year, Edward spent almost twice as much on the upkeep of his hunting dogs at Windsor.[28] David was moved to the Tower later that year.

David Bruce's treatment in 1357 also begs comparison with that of the captive King of France, Jean II. Jean was showered with gifts which make the relative poverty of David's stay all the more poignant. Sundry jewels were bought for him and his court for £525 while a short time later rings set with rubies and diamonds cost £231 alone.[29]

The upkeep of Charles, Duke of Orleans, is perhaps among the best-documented, sometimes alongside the Duke of Bourbon's upkeep:

To William Lovenye	£26 13s 4d
To Sir John Rothenhale	£20 14s – for wine sent to Pontefract
To Sir John Comberworth	£42 13s 4d
To Sir John Comberworth	£114 (in advance)
To Robert Watterton	£150
To Sir John Cornwall	£520
To John, Lord Fanhope	£ 66
To John Stourton	£ 95[30]

Towards the end of the period of Orleans's captivity the rate for his upkeep was 13s 4d per day. His captivity spanned the date, in 1424, after which captives were required to pay for their own upkeep. Certainly the duke's own efforts to provide for himself were considerable. The contemporary French historian Monstrelet suggested that, but for some greed and self-seeking among his jailers, Orleans might have been released sooner.

Even moving a court in exile or captivity, especially when their presence was in itself diplomatically sensitive, was costly. Each needed a guard. Moving the Duke of Bourbon from Portchester Castle (Hampshire) to Somerton Castle (Lincolnshire) in 1418 cost £10 in advance. Moreover when he was later moved to attend Henry V in France in 1421, three bodies of troops were needed:

> Robert Lord Paynyes – 4s per day and nineteen men at arms each paid at 12d per day and forty archers each paid at 6d per day;
> Sir Ralph Halsham – 2s per day and nine men at arms each paid at 12d per day and twenty archers each paid at 6d per day;
> Sir Thomas Hoo – 2s per day and nineteen men at arms each paid at 12d per day and forty archers each paid at 6d per day.[31]

On occasion even a dead exile or prisoner was afforded a guard. When the French hostage King Jean II died in England, Edward III paid out for an honour guard to accompany his body from London to Canterbury and Dover while further monies paid for Masses to be said for his soul at St Paul's, timed to coincide with his burial in France.[32] Edward was anxious to be seen by the Mother Church to have attended to every proper aspect of Jean's unfortunate death from natural causes, and not to attract any suspicion of wrongdoing.

Where wrongdoing was likely or certain, such as in the sudden death of the broken Henry VI in the Tower of London, even then there was a necessary dance of diplomatic etiquette. Its un-choreographed steps were carefully, if hastily, placed to divert at least some of the suspicion that someone had killed a king. It neither succeeded at the time nor with history's benefit of hindsight. As a result, the Duke of Gloucester, later Richard III, was hampered by suspicion of his guilt in the affair even before he became mixed up with the disappearances of the young princes in the Tower.

Ransom, Purchase & Exchange

After very successful battles it was usually the practice to buy and sell prisoners, not least because the individual captor was of insufficient rank and wealth to deal with his captive, and keep him in the manner to which he was accustomed until he could be ransomed. Thus Jean II, King of France, was captured at Poitiers in 1356 by Denis Morbeck, a Continental knight, but quickly sold to the Black Prince who acted on behalf of Edward III, so that a king held a king as was proper and no affront to chivalrous etiquette. Morbeck and all such captors, regardless of rank, were paid handsomely for their battle prowess and their prize, on the promise that ransom would recoup the expense to the treasury many times over. Fortunes were made in this way for ordinary soldiers and men-at-arms, as well as minor nobles. This was war booty for the enterprising, and circumstances rewarded the victor in battle handsomely. At the same Battle of Poitiers Sir Bartholomew de Burghershe captured the Count of Ventadour. Edward paid him 8,000 florins for his prisoner specifically to handle the ransom himself, as the count's position required.[33] It paid the Black Prince a huge compliment that he dealt so generously since the French king, expecting to win but finding his back to the proverbial wall, had himself famously declared (by flying the long orange oriflamme pennant) that no English prisoners would be taken. His victorious opponent's magnanimity might have been embarrassing but for the fact that he did not rub it in, but was entirely chivalrous and civil.

Captors were also paid for the expenses they incurred before they could deposit their prisoners. Thus Sir Nicholas Loveigne was paid half of a 10,000 mark ransom for the French knight Hugh de Chastillon in 1371, the rest to follow when the diplomacy was over.[34] Others stayed put, for one reason or another unable to be moved on. Thus Sir Roger de Beauchamp was paid for holding onto Charles de Blois when the official wording suggests he apparently wanted to be rid of him, probably because he was too hot to handle being of higher social status.[35]

Ransoms were usually paid. Not to do so was to break faith with the accepted code of chivalry which guided the conduct of the aristocracy. When Jean II's son broke faith, while standing in for his father who had returned to France to raise his own ransom, he brought shame on the royal house and Jean returned to England and captivity of his own accord, his dignity affronted. Occasionally circumstances conspired to prevent delivery but these were exceptional. In 1359, at the same time as Jean II's imprisonment, one William de Fifhyde from Dorset, taken by the French, returned home to raise his ransom but was then taken and imprisoned by his own side and relieved of his fortune in ransom, preventing his payment and with it compromising his honour.[36]

It was not always a simple matter of a period of exile coming to an end with a change of government. One man's (or woman's) regime might end, but advisors, courtiers and a jealous nobility could unbalance delicate negotiations or ensure that negotiation never really got underway. In such a way the Duke of Bedford ensured that the accession of Henry VI brought no end to the Duke of Orleans's ordeal. He continued to agitate against Orleans long after a peace party was in the ascendant.

Splits in a court might heal only slowly and a change in the man at the top was no guarantee of healing. In 1489 Henry VII, himself a former exile and a healer of the Wars of the Roses (in battle and in the ensuing peace), petitioned the Pope, Innocent VII, to intercede on behalf of Sir John Roos, who had been exiled as implicated in the murder of the Scots King James III. The letter asked for his exile to be reversed (as only the Church could overrule a king) and Sir John's lands restored to him by the new king, James IV.[37]

Divided by Faith

Woe betide the host who mistreated or neglected an exile or hostage. If this happened in wartime it might be expected that similar-ranked individuals on the other side might also be harmed or neglected. It was not unknown, however. While Charles of Orleans was a prisoner in a variety of host castles, largely being very well treated, his younger brother, the Duke of Bourbon, just a teenager when taken, was kept short of almost everything, including food, by his resentful hosts at Maxey Castle near Peterborough.

Across a religious divide, a chasm of misunderstanding at best and all-out antipathy or even hatred at worst, captives might expect the poorest of care, if not mistreatment. Thus the French king, Louis IX, captured in the Siege of Damietta on the Nile Delta in 1249/50, was poorly treated but it was nothing compared with many of his countrymen, even nobles, who were roughly handled, the wounded dispatched without care and the sick further damaged by deliberate and wilful harm and incarceration in terrible conditions. The historian Jean de Joinville almost died as one of these captives, taken to the point of he and his fellows confessing their sins to each other prior to execution, only to be spared at the last minute, Joinville because he was distantly related to the Holy Roman Emperor and therefore worth a ransom. He survived and told the woeful tale upon his release.

For those who were captured and lived to tell the tale, that tale could make the hearer's hair curl. It is our gain that Joinville himself was captured with his king, Louis IX of France, and left us his chronicles of the Sixth Crusade to relate the story of summary executions of prisoners and maltreatment or execution of the wounded as useless mouths to feed – although Saracen doctors and surgeons were among the best in the medieval world – so great was the mistrust and resentment of another culture along faith lines. That particular sword cut both ways and the numbers of prisoners who survived were comparatively few. On neither side was there seen to be any kudos in keeping an unbeliever alive. The maltreatment of prisoners (on both sides) went back so far that, by the end of the Third Crusade (1193), a pattern had emerged in which no one really expected to be given quarter and as a result few were.

There was a continuing fear of maltreatment on both sides, which could cause great uncertainty. Sultan Zizim was the younger brother of Sultan Bazajet of Turkey. Captured by the Christians in the 1480s after he fled a family coup which brought his brother to the throne, Zizim was for two years kept as the prisoner of the grand master of Rhodes. However, there were interests competing for his person, namely the Knights of Rhodes and a Hungarian Embassy. There was also interest from female French nobility, whose reasons for wishing his presence are unclear beyond the obvious amorous attentions of an exotic royal. He was in fact under the protection of the Church and held by Guy de Blanchefort, Prior of Auvergne at Bourganeuf Castle. Multiple negotiations took place and even English diplomats became involved through Sir John Kendal, Turcopolier. It was agreed that he might be moved to another castle closer to the sea, so long as it was under the jurisdiction of the Church, to await a Rhodian ship. In fact Zizim was not all that bothered so long as his eventual host did not turn him over to his brother Bazajet, of whom he was terrified after the coup. His intelligence was in fact badly flawed. Bazajet did not want his younger brother dead, but rather was all this time paying in cash and purported holy relics for his jailers to hang on to him somewhere, anywhere. His death would have been unthinkable, but out of sight, out of mind.[38] Zizim died not long after.

During the medieval period it remained the duty for all who could manage it to try to wrest control of the Holy Land from 'the unbelievers', 'the infidel', which translates as 'the unfaithful'. This duty manifested itself in the bitter and brutal struggle of the Crusades. They tied up armies for generations, drained national and private coffers and turned respectful combatants into embittered and hateful enemies whose warped, faith-driven vendetta lost its sense of purpose and all sense of reason.

To die in a crusade was to die alone, often of festering wounds but more often of dysentery or malaria, far from home, being buried in barely consecrated ground or left unburied as food for dogs and carrion. Thousands never even made it to their destination but died along the way, shipwrecked by Mediterranean storms, set upon by robbers and brigands or dead of bad food, even worse water or the lack of both. Most who set out on such a journey put their house in order before their departure. All wondered whether they would ever see home again. Lord Jean de Joinville, writing of his own departure to the Sixth Crusade in 1248–9, could not bear to look up, in a mixture of dread and anticipation, as his boat passed his home (and the inference of his waving wife and children) as he sailed down the River Rhone.[39]

It must be borne in mind too that a division by faith was not just between two religions but could be between two versions of the same faith. Around 1571 Queen Elizabeth is said to have composed a poem which highlighted Mary, Queen of Scots's threat to the spiritual well-being of her own subjects (let alone their physical well-being if there was a change of regime). There was considered to be a fine line indeed between spiritual well-being and physical, if one's authority was considered to be God-given.

The doubt of future foes
Exiles my present joy
And wit me warns to shun such snares
As threatens mine annoy.
For falsehood now doth flow
And subjects' faith doth ebb,
Which should not be if reason ruled
Or wisdom weaved the web.

The poem was said to have taken on a new lease of life after Mary's execution.

Boredom & Amusement

In the great medieval household the day was marked by some steady rhythms, which were carefully practised and in which everyone had their place and there was a place for everyone.

The year was marked for everyone by the great religious feasts and vigils and the Church observances that accompanied them all: prayer, feasting and fasting, abstinence and celebration. With only minor variations, these would have been kept by both hostage and host within the same household but with overlapping foci. Each had its lord, its own celebrant priests and its own secretaries, all rubbing shoulders in adjacent wings of the same house and in some cases each receiving its own supplies and cooking its own observant meals.[40]

From day to day the host and hostage or exiled court also matched each other, curtailed only by the necessary bookends of sunrise and sunset, in an age when natural light dictated the day and candle wax, if not a luxury in the households of the gentry, could still not be used up with profligacy. During the day, the household arose at dawn, its offices trammelled along lines of religious observance, meals (mainly with an eye to chivalry and etiquette towards their hosts or their charges) and the discussion and paperwork that went with the running of household affairs, and by extension, the running of estates back home.[41] In reality, though, such long-distance administration, in an age when travel was never faster than a well-shod horse or a ship in full sail before the wind, was effected by trusted stewards and seneschals. The efficacy of a noble court in exile or captivity was limited no more or less by distance than it was under normal circumstances. Exile for the estates back home began to bite more keenly when disputes could not be settled, taxes could not be apportioned and crops were not properly gathered in accordance with the accustomed smooth running of the estates. For a prisoner, hostage or exile, the normal decision-making regime at home was suspended for no one knew how long, and decisions taken could simply not be ratified and accorded the God-given authority they required in order to be accepted.

Despite clear routines, the lot of the exile and the captive, however wealthy in their own country, was rarely free from at least some boredom despite the receipt of gifts from home, however regular or genuinely well chosen. The restricted pastimes of the principal subjects of this book are related in each relevant chapter. However, there was limited opportunity for most exiles to amuse themselves since their funds were limited by their circumstances except for those whose diplomacy, desperate or not, brought some reward.

For those who managed to secure funds as well as gifts from home and whose honour was assured against escape attempts, some semblance of normality could be purchased and hawking, hunting and entertainments were continued in their enforced abode, often putting further pressure on their hosts whose homes were usually considered their own preserve. For Jean II, the French royal court in exile was essentially that, simply on an extended progress. Except in times of English national alarm, embassies still came and went. Ambassadors were received, royal and noble guests entertained and the exiles themselves travelled about to be entertained. Edward III was at particular pains to extend every expected hospitality to his guest.

Close confinement was not always the end of amusement however much Mary, Queen of Scots might have disagreed. In 1506 a Venetian agent wrote to the Senate of Venice and related how Duke Valentino (the infamous Cesare Borgia), held imprisoned in Medina del Campo, amused himself by flying his falcons from his balcony, provided and fed by money sent by his brother-in-law, the King of Navarre.[42]

Thanks, Memory & Hope

Edward IV, although he was in Bruges for only three months, did not forget the reception the city gave him. He wrote to them in glowing terms from Canterbury on 29 May 1471, his trials and tribulations behind him, addressing them in personal as well as official cordiality, 'To each of you, greetings and affection! Dear and special friends, we thank you, with our greatest cordiality, for the good cheer and great courtesy you paid us … when we spent time in your city.'[43]

It is perhaps, however, more to be expected that former exiles might wish to forget their ill fortune and the time spent torn from their lives. Most royals who returned to either reclaim their thrones or in some way regain their station chose to bury the unhappy past thereafter, perhaps understandably living most days as if each was to be their last. The swift third marriage of Charles, Duke of Orleans, on his return from English exile can hardly have wiped away twenty-five years from his memory but it went a long way to laying entirely new foundations for his new life.

For those whose lives would be broken, their despair and self-pity is perhaps summed up in the short poem by an Italian cleric, imprisoned in Bologna in 1362: 'Since fortune so cruelly cast me down. I pray to you, Death, earnestly, to end these sorry tears.'[44]

For the medieval Italian poet, Dante Aligheri, his own twenty-year exile in a succession of North Italian cities was summed up in his own lines: 'You'll find how salty it tastes, other people's bread, how hard it is, going up, down other people's stairs.'[45]

For Thomas Mowbray, Duke of Norfolk, in 1397 and Faulkes de Bréauté before him around 1225, death did indeed end their tears of self-pity, each dying broken men far from home. Charles I felt he was living only the husk or shell of life in his incarceration. Mary, Queen of Scots too had been hardly any more enamoured of her protracted stretch. Charles's 'few steps' between the prisons and graves of princes (see above), were short and liable to be taken at short notice. He and others, despite escape attempts both bold and risible, had good reason to feel melancholic, expecting their incarceration to end (in Geltner's words) 'in a coroner's cart'.[46]

For the confident and the hopeful, release or return was no more than they expected. Richard I wasted no time in racing back to England to set his affairs in order and reproach his brother John's much reviled regime, which had bled England dry in his absence. Within a few weeks of his return he was back in the field of battle seeking to strengthen and hold Normandy against the French, which he did for a further five years.

Edward IV never lost sight of his royal right to rule, whatever the perceived legitimacy of the Yorkist cause and claim to the English throne. His return in 1471 was planned far better than his hasty flight in 1470. Buoyed up by money from the Duke of Burgundy, his cause was suddenly financed in a way that the likes of Charles II lacked from beginning to end. Money could buy a return and could moderate the terms of exile and imprisonment. Jean II never went short of cash in England, be it from France or from his chivalrously deferent and respectful captors, Edward III and Edward the Black Prince.

Jean II cited the biblical parallel of the children of Israel in exile, asking bitterly before his partying hosts, 'How can I sing the Lord's song in a strange land?' In a very religious Europe each would have been aware that Christ their Saviour too began his life as an exile, a refugee in Egypt, fleeing Herod's persecution of the firstborns.[47] It was of some comfort to the medieval Christian mind to be able to share Christ's suffering. So too the possibility of a divinely inspired end to their incarceration had its biblical precedents in St Peter and St Paul.[48]

For many of the later subjects in this book (at least Edward IV onwards), the great exiled wanderers of a classical past were either well known or becoming known thanks to the opening up of classical literature during the Renaissance. The experiences (or adventures) of Odysseus became better known but it was Aeneas, the mythical hero of Vergil and also taken up by Dante, who increasingly captured the noble imagination. His ultimately hopeful exile, borne out of the despair of the sack of his beloved Troy, and justified by its Roman end, might be a blueprint for what many in a similar position might wish for:

> So at length I turn back to my friends, and here with wonder find new comrades, a vast concourse, matrons, men, an army massed for exile – piteous throng! – From all sides gathered, armed in heart and gear, wherever I list to lead them over the sea.[49]

For Aeneas, Troy was not rebuilt in a day and exile and imprisonment might be treated as a new beginning and a preparation for a new life to come. Adventure, the hope of a return and the distant promise of release kept exiles, hostages and prisoners alive.

NOTES

Introduction

1 Soden, Iain, *Ranulf de Blondeville: The First English Hero* (Stroud: Amberley Books, 2009).
2 Luke 4:18.

1 A Caged Lion: Richard I in Austria & Germany (1192–94)

1 Stubbs (1864, 419), where Richard's preparations and departure are related.
2 Wm Newburgh in Howlett (1884, 382); Roger of Hoveden III in Stubbs (1870, 195).
3 Hoveden, *ibid.* 'iuxta Wenam, in villa viciniori, in domo despecta captivavit'.
4 The dating of Richard's captivity follows Landon's work on his charters (1935) and Richard's letters in Stubbs (1865). The chroniclers mainly concern themselves with the red-letter days, such as his capture, etc.
5 Wm of Newburgh in Howlett (1884, 386) 'tenebatur in vinculis'.
6 Stubbs (1864, 444) 'Ille rex inclitus tractatur indignis, et si non vinculis sed ineptis custodiis'.
7 Felix Fabri, a German friar, writing in 1484 and cited on this observation by Geltner (2008, 71–2).
8 Hoveden in Stubbs (1870, 204) '[John] … affirmans quod rex Angliae frater suus mortuus erat'.
9 *Ibid.* (1870, 198).
10 *Ibid.* 'qui cum totam Alemanniam peregrassent, et regem non invenissent, Baveriam ingressi sunt, et obviaverunt regi

in villa quae dicitur Oxefer, ubi ducebatur ad imperatorem, habiturus cum eo colloquium in die Palmarum'.
11 *Ibid.* 'eleganter, prudenter'.
12 Letter in Stubbs (1865, 362–3), for example.
13 Hoveden in Stubbs (1870, 211) 'carissimus noster illustris Rex Ricardus'.
14 *Ibid.* (1870, 225–6).
15 *Ibid.* (1870, 206) 'mandavit, et facta sunt universa'.
16 Hoveden in Stubbs (1870, 234–5) for the nobles and churchmen listed.
17 *Ibid.* (1870, 233) 'omnes qui aderant prae gaudio lacrymati sunt'.
18 *Ibid.* (1870, 233) 'Alan Trenchemer, ut cum confacilius tansiret inter insulas; singulis autem noctibus exiens de galea illa intravit navem magnam et pulcherrimam, quae venerat de Rie, et in ea iacuit in nocte'.
19 Hoveden in Stubbs (1870, 276–7) 'ut cum militibus suis luderet, cecidit equus suus sper eum, et confregit pedem eius'.
20 See Soden (2009, 25–6) for the siege.

2 A King's Ransom: Jean II of France in England (1356–60, 1363–64)

1 John Capgrave, edited by Hingeston (1858, 217), whose tally was in agreement with that of Thomas Walsingham (Riley 1863, 283); the exact numbers may be disputed, however. A monk of Malmesbury (Haydon 1863) related fourteen earls and twenty-one lords captured, twenty-two dead; 1,400 knights captured and 3,000 men-at-arms, with 2,500 cavalry dead.

However he noted that innumerable foot soldiers were killed.

2 Eventually this much-disputed honour was settled on a knight from St Omer, Denis Morbek, who was represented in England unusually by a woman advocate Matilda Rous as related in the Pell Records, ed. Devon (1837, 180).

3 Hewitt (1958, 133–4).

4 A metaphor used at the time by Thomas Walsingham in Riley (1863, 283): France became 'gens sine capite'.

5 My list here is compiled from a dozen different chroniclers, commentators and records. Many went unnamed by the chroniclers. It was later ironic that the unlucky Count d'Eu, captured a second time at the Battle of Nicopolis (1396), died while the hostage of the Turk, Sultan Bajazet (Froissart).

6 Monk of Malmesbury in Haydon (1863, 225).

7 'acceptus est a clero honorifice, atque civibus cum omni gaudio et honore', Thomas Walsingham in Riley (1863, 283).

8 Pell Records in Devon (1837, 166).

9 The Black Prince's Register in Dawes (1933, Vol IV: 254, 333).

10 *Ibid.* (254).

11 Pell Records in Devon (1837, 165–6).

12 Pope Innocent IV, in Bliss and Johnson (1897, 619–20). Cardinal Talleyrand had been working with and, in all probability, against Edward III since the 1340s, so was a practised diplomat. Edward was unlikely to have been moved by any of the cardinal's pleas, since the Pope wanted only a united Anglo-French leadership against the Muslim east. Their national territorial ambitions were a constant distraction: see Haines (1989, 223–4) and, generally, Zacour (1960).

13 Zacour (1960, 52).

14 Bliss and Johnson (1897, 623); Longueville stayed, but was later exchanged as one of Jean II's hostages in 1360.

15 Tout (1930, 346–7 n7).

16 The Black Prince's Register in Dawes (1933, Vol IV: 253).

17 Monk of Malmesbury (1863, 225); John Capgrave in Hingeston (1858, 218); Talleyrand and his fellow cardinal stayed in Church-owned premises in London (Zacour (1960, 56–7).

18 The translation is mine, from Thomas Walsingham in Riley (1863, 283).

19 Pell Records in Devon (1837, 168).

20 Numerous instances in Bond (1853, 457–462).

21 The efforts of cardinals Talleyrand and Albano, Papal Nuncios in Bliss and Johnson (1897, 626).

22 The description is by Hewitt (1958 [2004], 93). With his own reasonable claim to the French throne, he had already plotted to overthrow Jean II in 1355–6, prompting his own arrest at Rouen in April 1356.

23 Most payments for jewels were only made when Jean was finally released (and the money began to come in), for which see the more than 3,000 marks in the Pell Records for November 1362, ed. Devon (1837, 176).

24 Calendar of Patent Rolls 31 Edw. III: pt II; m7, m24, 25 (May, June, August 1357); modern French sources put the court at fifty servants, a jester, three doctors and a priest-confessor. However, others are known by name whose standing make them more than just servants and the figure is likely to have been larger. His court painter, a furrier, spicer and confectioner are all well attested, some by name.

25 Devoisse (1985), who also describes Jean II as quick-tempered and confrontational, not a description which was easily recognisable during his captivity in England, when his demeanour was of one who exhibits only calm.

26 The Black Prince's Register in Dawes (1933, 254, 333).

27 From July 1354 Margaret de Manny was held there 'as quietly and honourably' as possible (Patent Rolls).

28 Calendar of Patent Rolls 33 Edw. III: pt I; m14d, 24 March 1359.

29 Andrews (1947, 27–46) following their original publication by the Duc d'Aumale and Douët d'Arcq (1851).

30 For Jean's meetings with Abbot Thomas see Riley (1865: II, 407–9). The original letters do not survive, only the near contemporary chronicle.

31 Talleyrand had been instrumental in confirming Thomas's appointment to St Albans, when politics threatened to derail his candidacy (Zacour 1960, 16). Their meeting at St Albans is recorded in Riley (1865: II, 385).

32 Zacour (*ibid.* appendix).

33 Calendar of Patent Rolls 33 Edw. III: pt II; m16, 26–27 July 1359.

34 For the king's expenses in detail, see le Duc d'Aumale (1856) and Doran (1857). They are not calendared, nor do they break down by period of residence.

35 Calendar of Patent Rolls 33 Edw. III: pt III; m5, 18 Dec 1359.

36 Calendar of Patent Rolls 1 March 1360, m28; Calendar of Close Rolls 34 Edw. III: pt I; m22d 8 March 1360; The Black Prince's Register in Dawes (1933, 345).

37 VCH Hertfordshire II 168–9.

38 For the death in custody see Rodney and Chapman (1937, 129, no. 362); for the lack of crops after eleven years see The Black Prince's Register in Dawes (1933, 353).

39 For the jewellery payments in November 1362 see the Pell Records in Devon (1837, 176).

40 'Eo tempore, in Anglia plures homines, bestiae, et arbores, violenti fulgure perierunt; et diabolus in humana specie apparens locutus est', Walsingham in Riley (1863, 290).

41 This extraordinarily full list was first given by Thomas Walsingham, for which see Riley (*ibid.*). According to Froissart, the hapless de Couci died a hostage alongside the Cout de Eu after the battle of Nicopolis (see note 3 above).

42 For the petitions to Urban V, see Bliss and Twemlow (1902). It was suggested that two others should stand in Robert de St Venant's place.

43 *Ibid.* (1902, 35, 38 & 39).

44 Pell Records in Devon (1837, 177); Calendar of Patent Rolls 33 Edw. III, Pt 1, 6 Feb 1359.

45 Foissart in Jolliffe (1968, 184).

46 Psalm 137.

47 Pell Records in Devon (1837, 181–2).

48 Events most simply set out by John Capgrave in Hingeston (1858, 222).

49 18–19 April 1364 in Devon (1837, 183).

50 *Ibid.* (1837, 190–2). Although by then many may not have been 'leftovers' of Poitiers, Devon (1835, 394, 429) shows negotiations ongoing in 1370 for French hostages being held in Warwickshire, Leicestershire, Nottinghamshire, Derbyshire, Lichfield and Coventry.

3 'Alas I Am Alone!' Charles, Duke of Orleans, in England (1415–40)

1 The best list of the foremost prisoners is given by Monstrelet in Johnes (1845) I: 346.

2 Rymer's Foedera IX 334, (April 1416).

3 Pell Records, the Issue Rolls of the Exchequer in Devon (1837, 344).

4 Rymer's Foedera IX, 337, 339, 369, 432.

5 Macleod (1969, 136).

6 Rymer's Foedera IX 423.

7 Macleod (1969, 144).

8 Rymer's Foedera IX 455–6.

9 Macleod (1969, 140).

10 Devon (1837, 352–3).

11 Devon (1835, xlix–l).

12 Rymer's Foedera IX, 801.

13 Devon (1837, 363).

14 Monstrelet in Johnes (1845, I: 459).

15 *Ibid.* I: 477–8.

16 Devon (1837, 383).

17 Macleod (1969, 163).

18 Rymer's Foedera X, 350.

19 1 Mark = 13s 4d, or two-thirds of a pound, apparently the standard daily allowance for his prisoner. The 1432 expenses payment in Devon (1837, 413).

20 For which in detail see Monstrelet in Johnes (1845) vol. I.

21 Macleod (1969, 187); Macleod also states that William was instinctively a Francophile, but this surely rather overlooks such leanings amongst much of the Anglo-French court of England. Despite the war, links across the channel remained strong and widespread, although the 1430s saw a big dip in trading relations.

22 *Ibid.* 208–13.

23 In May nine of his servants were given safe conduct passes to go to France in aid of the money-raising, Rymer's Foedera X, 665.

24 Macleod (1969, 224); the other likely occasion was Charles's visit to Peterborough, while Jean was at Maxey around 1421–2.

25 Devon (1837, 450).

26 Twemlow (1909, 222).

27 Devon (1837, 439).

28 Their union would produce King Louis XI of France. As late as 1498 negotiations were still ongoing with Louis for the outstanding balance of Charles's ransom (Brown 1864, 271; no 771).

29 Monstrelet (1845, II: 100).

4 The Company of Friends: Edward IV in Bruges (1470–71)

1 Correspondence in Brown (1864, 121); (Hinds 1912, 123–4).
2 Habington (1640, 61).
3 Brown (1864, 123).
4 *Ibid.* (124).
5 *Ibid.* (125).
6 Dormer-Harris (1907–13, II: 358–9).
7 Many modern historians follow the story of an Olney capture, but there is a ring of truth about the trap supposedly sprung at Coventry, for which see Jehan de Wavrin in Hardy and Hardy (1891, 584–5); as a chronicler, Jehan de Wavrin was in the pay of the Earl of Warwick and so had nothing to gain by confusing the story in this case.
8 Hinds (1912, 142).
9 *Ibid.* (1912, 143).
10 Halliwell (1839, 11).
11 Habington (1640, 66).
12 For the exact dating in Flanders, Béhault de Dornan (1931).
13 *Ibid.* (1931, 13, n2).
14 Scafield (1923) in Béhault de Dornan (1931, 138).
15 Jehan de Wavrin in Hardy and Hardy (1891, 655). St Anne is a saint renowned for her literary leanings. Edward's devotions continued, and culminated in miraculous goings-on on Palm Sunday 1471 at Daventry Priory, Northamptonshire (*ibid.* 1891, 655–6). All this lent credence to the assumption of St Anne's help and favour to a cultured man of letters to regain the throne, and sat well with Edward's image with the likes of Caxton and Louis de Gruuthuse.
16 Habington (1640, 68–9).
17 Polydore Vergil in Ellis (1844, 133).
18 Neilson (1930, xiii).
19 Brown (1864, 125).
20 Vaughan (1973, 71), citing Henrard (1875, 46, n1).
21 Habington (1640, 73).
22 Abram (1917, 218).
23 Béhault de Dornan (1931, 140).
24 Halliwell (1839, 13).
25 Bruce (1838, 1).
26 Hinds (1912, 150).
27 Letter to Bruges 29 May 1471 in Béhault de Dornan (1931, 147–8), Decree by Venetian Senate in Brown (1864, 126–7).

5 Rooms with No View: Henry VI in the Tower (1471) & Henry Tudor (Henry VII) in Brittany (1471–85)

1 Polydore Vergil in Ellis (1844, 108).
2 *Warkworth Chronicle* in Halliwell (1839, 5).
3 Polydore Vergil in Ellis (1844, 111–5).
4 Halliwell (1839, 5).
5 Devon (1837, 489).
6 *Ibid.* (1837, 495 & 497).
7 *Ibid.* 497.
8 In Bruce 1838.
9 In Halliwell 1839.
10 Brown (1864, 128; no. 434).
11 Devon (1837, 495 & 497)
12 Halliwell (1839, xiii–xv); a murder weapon would have marked the body, but the bleeding nose after death might indicate a haemorrhagic poison, but not of course the poisoner. Alternatively the dramatic observation may simply be the result of poor embalming techniques.
13 *Chronicle of London* (ed. C. L. Kingsford, 185).
14 Devon (1837, 495–6).
15 Devon (1837, 498).
16 Polydore Vergil in Ellis (1844, 152).
17 Polydore Vergil in Ellis (1844, 134–5).
18 *Ibid.* (1844, 164).
19 Brown (1864, 129; no. 437).
20 Polydore Vergil in Ellis (1844, 155).
21 *Ibid.* (155); Oration of Duke Francis by Bernard Andrea Tholosate in Gardner (1858, 17–18) 'hic adulescentulus princeps' (the writer uses a playful and perhaps rather dismissive diminutive); 'illum manu gratiose apprehendens, in regnam suam cum magna hilaritate perduxit'. The laughter was probably genuine for the moment.
22 Habington (1640, 112).
23 *Ibid.* (1640, 113).
24 Polydore Vergil in Ellis (1844, 158).
25 Habington (1640, 113).
26 Polydore Vergil in Ellis (1844, 159).
27 Habington (1640, 113–4).
28 Polydore Vergil in Ellis (1844, 164).
29 Habington (1640, 173–4).
30 Polydore Vergil in Ellis (1844, 164).
31 Habington (1640, 213).
32 Polydore Vergil in Ellis (1844, 201).
33 *Ibid.* (1844, 216).

6 'En Ma Fin Est Mon Commencement': Mary, Queen of Scots in England (1568–87)

1 'In my end is my beginning'. These prescient words were embroidered on Mary's bed canopy throughout her confinement. In fact they were adopted from her mother, Mary of Guise, whose motto it was previously. It presaged the claim of her own son, James, to the throne of England.

2 I am grateful to my friend Rachel Swallow for taking copious notes at a British Library exhibition of original letters and documents from Mary's final years when illness prevented my attendance (referred to as BL hereafter). To Sallie Gee go my profound thanks for her editing and suggestions for this whole chapter.

3 Cheetham (1987), 52.

4 I am only too aware of my shortcomings in my understanding across the gender divide. My thanks go to Sallie and to Rachel for their help.

5 BL: Cotton MS Caligula Ci, f.218.

6 BL: Cotton MS Caligula Ci, f.97.

7 Leader (1880) 4, 9.

8 *Ibid*. 18.

9 *Ibid*. 24.

10 *Ibid*. 44. Leader's narrative is followed hereon for the most part.

11 Leader (1880), 97.

12 *Ibid*. 180–83.

13 *Arquebusier*: in the most basic sense, an early rifleman.

14 *Ibid*. 228.

15 Leader (1880), 298–302.

16 *Ibid*. 352.

17 *Ibid*. 371.

18 *Ibid*. 478.

19 *Ibid*. 480.

20 Mackie (1832), 223.

21 From the papers of Ralph Sadler.

22 Correspondence: Elizabeth to Sadler, 12 August 1584. BL: Collection of Mark Piggott OBE.

23 Leader (1880), 609–13.

24 Correspondence: Robert Dudley, Earl of Leicester, to Sir Francis Walsingham, 24 Dec 1584. BL: Collection of Mark Piggott OBE.

25 BL: Collection of Mark Piggott OBE.

26 *Ibid*.

27 *Ibid*. Correspondence: Elizabeth to Sadler, 11 January 1585.

28 *Ibid*. Correspondence: Burghley to Sadler, 18 January 1585.

29 *Ibid*. Correspondence: Walsingham to Sadler, 19 March 1585.

30 *Ibid*. Correspondence: Elizabeth to Sadler, 10 April 1585.

31 BL: Egerton MS 2124, f.36.

32 Colvin (1975), 250.

7 Intrigue & the Would-Be Escaper: Charles I in England (1646–48)

1 Hinds 1926, 298 (doc. 470).

2 Herbert 1815, 14; stops at Durham, Richmond, Ripon, Leeds, Nottingham and Leicester. Hinds relates diplomatic notice of the stage-management (1926, 305, doc. 486).

3 *Ibid*. 8–9; Herbert lists at least nineteen in the court.

4 Venetian agents even reported the disguise was that of a fisherman and noted his subsequent torture – Hinds 1926, 314 (doc. 509).

5 Herbert 1815, 19.

6 Journals of the House of Lords, IX, 80, 193–4.

7 Bowle (1975) says 500 horses (after the Venetian spies – Hinds 1926, 320–1, doc. 523) but I follow the contemporary report of Edward Hyde (Huehns 1979, 290–1). It suited the Venetians to overplay the king's rough treatment.

8 Huehns 1979, 291.

9 Hinds 1927, 32, 34 (docs 64, 78).

10 Hinds 1927, 39 (doc 78–9); Herbert 1815, 95–7.

11 Herbert 1815, 60; Hillier 1852, 81 cites Herbert.

12 Hillier 1852, 100. It is possible that this was an inspiration for the famous Colditz escape attempt of the Second World War.

13 *Ibid*. 99, 102–3. Notes were also placed in the king's gloves, which were held during meals by a trusted servant.

14 *Ibid*. 108–12.

15 Hillier 1852, 140.

16 Hinds 1927, 71, 72, 80 (docs 173, 175, 208).

17 Hinds 1927, 83 (doc. 222); Herbert 1815, 122–3.

18 Herbert 1815, 124, 127.

19 Gauden 1649 (1869 edition), 216, 242.

20 Herbert 1815, 68; letter to Princess Elizabeth 14 Oct 1648.
21 Gauden 1649 (1869 edition), 244.

8 Outstaying One's Welcome: Prince Charles (Charles II) in Bruges (1656–58)

1 Letter dated at Vienna 11 Dec 1655 in Hinds (1930, 153).
2 Communicated by the Venetian secretary in England in *ibid.* (191).
3 From the Venetian Ambassador to France to the Doge of Venice 6 April 1656 in *ibid.* (155).
4 Hinds (1930, 204); Behault de Dornan (1931, 164).
5 Letter in French dated Paris 21 April 1656, in the possession of Philip, Lord Hardwicke, Lord High Chancellor, translated within twenty-four hours for Sir John Thurloe, Secretary of State, both in London. Thurloe Papers xxxvii, 281 on www.british-history.ac.uk.
6 Béhault de Dornan (1931, 174).
7 *Ibid.* (174–7). Much of the block is relatively unchanged today, although the House of Seven Towers is gone.
8 Hinds (1930, 211).
9 16 June 1656, *Ibid.* (232).
10 Mother Augustine was born Lady Helen Bedingfield. The Bruges house had been founded out of an English Carmelite house in Anvers in 1629 and was known as the house of 'Les Dames Anglaises' (Béhault de Dornan 1931, 383). The Bedingfield family were loyal royalists and had already lost a small fortune backing Charles I and his exiled son.
11 Béhault de Dornan (1931, 173).
12 For the list see Steinman (1853, 346), quoting guild records; for the arrow, Béhault de Dornan (1931, 340).
13 For the duke's arrival see Béhault de Dornan (1931, 172); for his delay in Paris, Hinds (1930, 212).
14 Béhault de Dornan (1931, 363).
15 In Belgium in Béhault de Dornan (1931, 165–8) and in England in Steinman (1853, 335–49) both partly from Bruges's civic and guild-related records.
16 Steinman (*Ibid.* 340–2).
17 Hinds (1930, 263).
18 Bruges, in mercantile decline, had no direct link to the sea since 1520, when silt closed the Zwin estuary, choking off Bruges's seaport. This was the single

biggest topographical change since Edward IV's stay in 1470–1, and one which made Bruges's mercantile economy all the more fragile.
19 Hinds (1930, 263).
20 Extract from a letter in Thompson (1878, 14).
21 Francesco Giavarina in Hinds (1930, 284).
22 *Ibid.* (239, 246).
23 Hinds (1931, 125).
24 Warner (1920, 4).
25 Béhault de Dornan (1931, 212): 'Toute sa cour séjourna avec une pompe toute royale.' In fact on this matter Béhault de Dornan faces none of the difficult social aspects of these two years. He unashamedly tries to suggest Charles passed his time in a state of calm, but 'sought to lose himself' because of his deep unhappiness at his exile. He can bring himself to say nothing more of the debauchery but paints a wholly fanciful picture of a pensive monarch in waiting, taking long walks in his garden.
26 Warner (1920, 13).
27 He would later become the rebel James, Duke of Monmouth and Buccleuch.
28 *Ibid.* (34).
29 Hinds (1931, 29).
30 Hutton (1989, 124).
31 Steinman (1835, 340).
32 Warner (1920, 43).
33 It must be borne in mind that the recent history of Flanders had suffered from as much religious bloodshed in the late 16th century as England had in the same period. Bruges itself had also been besieged over religious matters as recently as 1630. Sensibilities ran very deep.
34 Béhault de Dornan (1931, 398, 400).
35 *Ibid.* (402–3).
36 Béhault de Dornan (1931, 403).
37 *Ibid.* 'le culte anglican célébré secrètement'.
38 Warner (1920, 70–1).
39 *Ibid.* (1920, 105).
40 *Ibid.* (114).
41 Francesco Giavinara reported his coming and going in Hinds (1931, 246).
42 Warner (1920, 138).
43 *Ibid.* (188).

9 Ordinary Lives, Extraordinarily Lived

1 Polydore Vergil in Ellis (1844, 135).
2 Habington (1640, 61).
3 *Ibid.* (1640, 230).

4 *Ibid.* (1640, 231).

5 Soden (2009, 137, n18); Thompson (1895, 211).

6 Zimmern 1891, 222–32 for the rise to power of Gustav Vasa.

7 Thomas Walsingham in Riley (1864, 226; 241; 247).

8 Soden (2009, 100–3) for the circumstances.

9 The terms of the banishment cited by Bruce (1999, 188).

10 Brown (1864, 38; no. 128) for the galley; *ibid.* (47–8; no. 166) for the debt; Thomas Walsingham in Riley (1864, 230) for his wife's consequent death.

11 John Capgrove in Hingeston (1858, 147); see most recently Everard (2000) or Soden (2009) for her colourful family circumstances and her pivotal role in claims to the Duchy of Brittany. For more than a quarter of a century, she was too important to set free.

12 Hewitt (1958, 95).

13 Bond (1853, 467).

14 Devon 1837, various, 131–78 (1317–64).

15 Calendar of Patent Rolls 26 July 1354.

16 Calendar of Inquisitions Misc. in Rodney and Chapman (1937, 129; no. 362).

17 Devon (1837, 379).

18 Devon (1835, xlix).

19 *Ibid.* (1835, 394 & 429).

20 William Cecil to his son Robert *c*. 1580. 'Certain precepts for the well ordering of a man's life', *Advice to a son*, 9.

21 Bishop Overton to Earl of Shrewsbury 12 Oct 1590, in Starkey 1990 (ed.).

22 Juana was sister to Katherine of Aragon, both daughters of King Ferdinand of Aragon. At the time Katherine was married to her first husband, Prince Arthur, doomed heir to the English throne. In her widowhood she would later marry his brother, the future Henry VIII, the marriage of boredom at the heart of the English Reformation.

23 Brown (1864, 326, doc. 890); for the shipwreck *ibid.* (p. 311 doc. 864).

24 Devon (1837, 271).

25 Devon (1837, 374).

26 *Ibid.* (1837, 151).

27 *Ibid.* (384).

28 Devon (1837, 163).

29 *Ibid.* (1837, 176).

30 All Devon (1837).

31 *Ibid.* (352, 363).

32 *Ibid.* (183).

33 Devon (1835, xliii).

34 *Ibid.* (1835, 445).

35 *Ibid.* (1835, 394).

36 Close Rolls 33 Edw. III, pt III; m5d.

37 Brown (1864, 177, doc. 549).

38 Brown (1864, 166, 172, docs 522, 533).

39 Joinville in Johnes 1848 (1807 translation).

40 Woolgar (1999, 91).

41 *Ibid.* (1999, 89–95).

42 Devon (1837, 306 no. 890).

43 Given in full in the French in (among others) Béhault de Dornan (1931, 147).

44 Reproduced and translated in Geltner (2008, 114).

45 Paradise: XVII, 58–60. Translated by Steve Ellis.

46 Geltner (2008, 74).

47 Luke 2, 13–23.

48 Acts 12, 1–19 for Peter; 16, 22–40 for Paul.

49 Vergil, Aeneid: II, 795–800. Translated by James Rhoades.

BIBLIOGRAPHY

Abram A, 1917 Military service in a Flemish commune: Bruges 1288–1480, *History* I, 215–21

Allmund C T, (ed.) 1972 Anglo-French negotiations of 1439, *Camden Miscellany 24*, Camden Society 4th Series 9

Andrews H C, 1947 *The Chronicles of Hertford Castle*, Hertford

Ashton R, 1994 *Counter-revolution – the second Civil War and its origins 1646–8*, Yale UP

Aumale, le Duc d', 1856 The prisoners of Poitiers, *Gentleman's Magazine*, New Series October 1856, 452–9

Baum, J 1956 German Cathedrals, London, Thames and Hudson

Behault de Dornon, A de, 1931 *Bruges séjour d'exil des rois d'Angleterre Edouard IV (1471) et Charles II (1656–1658)*, Bruges

Bevan B, 2000 *Henry VII, the first Tudor King*

Bliss W H, and Johnson C, (ed.) 1897 *Calendar of Papal Registers; Papal Letters, III: 1342–62*, Rolls Series, HMSO

Blyth J D, 1961 The battle of Tewkesbury, *Transactions of the Bristol and Gloucestershire Archaeological Society*, 80, 99–120

Bond E A, 1853 Notices of the last days of Isabella, Queen of Edward the Second, drawn from an account of the expenses of her household, *Archaeologia* 35, 453–69

Bowle J, 1975 *Charles the First*, London

Broome D M, (ed.) 1926 The ransom of John II, King of France, 1360–1370, *Camden Miscellany 14*, Camden Society

Brouwers D D, (ed.) 1905–6 *Memoires de J de Haymin 1465–77*, Liege

Brown R, (ed.) 1864 *Calendar of State Papers and Manuscripts relating to English Affairs existing in the archives and collections of Venice and other libraries of Northern Italy: 1, (1202–1509)*, Longmans, London

Bruce M L, 1999 *The Usurper King: Henry of Bolingbroke 1366–99*, Rubicon, London

Bruce J, (ed.) 1838 *The historie of the arrival of Edward IV in England and the final recoverye of his Kingdomes from Henry VI, AD 1471, better known as The Fleetwood Chronicle*, Camden Society Publications 1.

Burne A H, 1938 The Battle of Poitiers, *English Historical Review 53*, 21–52

Calmette J, and Durville G, (ed.) 1924–5 *'Memoires' de Philippe de Commynes*, 3 Vols, Paris

Chaplais P, (ed.) 1952 Some documents regarding the fulfillment and interpretation of the Treaty of Brétigny 1361–1369, *Camden Miscellany 19*, Camden Society

Chapman H, 1964 *The tragedy of Charles II*, London

Cheetham J K, 1987 *Mary Queen of Scots: the captive years*, Sheffield

Cole H, 1976 *The Black Prince*, Purnell: Abingdon

Colvin H M, 1975 *The history of the King's works: II (Medieval)*

Colvin H M, 1975 *The history of the King's works: III* (1485–1660) pt 1

Colvin H M, 1982 *The history of the King's works: IV* (1485–1660) pt 2

Cussons J E, 1874 *History of Hertfordshire: Hundred of Hertford*

Dawes M C B, (ed.) 1933 *Register of Edward the Black Prince preserved in the PRO: I–IV;* (IV: England 1351–1365), HMSO London

Delachenal R, 1916 *Les grandes chroniques de France : chroniques des règnes de Jean II et de Charles V*, Paris

Devoisse J,1985 *Jean le Bon*, Paris

Devon F, (ed.) 1835 *Pell Records. Issue Roll of Thomas de Brantingham, 44 Edward III (1370)*, London

Devon F, (ed.) 1837 *Pell Records. Issues of the Exchequer: a collection of payments made out of his majesty's revenue: Henry III-Henry VI inclusive*, London

Doran J, 1857 Journal of the Expenses of John, King of France, in England 1359–60, *Notes and Queries*: V , (135), 505–6

Dormer-Harris M, 1907–13 *The Coventry Leet Book*

Douet d'Arcq M L, 1851 *Comptes de l'Argenterie des Rois de France au XIVème siècle*, Société de l'Histoire de France, Paris

Ellis H, (ed.) 1844 *Three books of Polydore Vergil's English History*, Camden Society 1st Series 29

Emerson B, 1976 *The Black Prince*, Wiedenfield and Nicholson, London

Gairdner J, (ed.) 1858 *Memorials of Henry VII: Historia Regis Henrici Septimi a Bernado Andrea Tholosate conscripta*, Longmans, London

Gardiner S R, 1893 *History of the Great Civil War 1642–1649*, 4 vols

Gauden J, 1649 (1869 edn) *Eikon Basilike or The Pourtraiture of his Sacred Majestie in his solitudes and sufferings*, London

Geltner G, 2008 *The medieval prison, a social history*, Princeton University Press, Oxford

Habington W, 1640 *The historie of Edward the fourth, king of England*, London

Haines R M, 1989 *Ecclesia Anglicana: studies in the English church of the later middle ages*, Toronto

Halliwell J O, (ed.) 1839 *A chronicle of the first thirteen years of the reign of King Edward the fourth by J Warkworth*, Camden Society 1st series 10

Hardy W, and Hardy E, (ed.) 1891 *Receuil des Chroniques et anciennes istoires de la Grand Bretagne a present nomme Engleterre par Jehan de Wavrin, seigneur de Forestal* Kraus Reprint 1967

Harriss G L, and Harriss MA, 1972 John Benet's Chronicle 1400–62, *Camden Miscellany* 24; Camden Society 4th Series, 9

Hay D (ed.) 1950 *The Anglia Historia of Polydore Vergil 1485–1537*, Camden Society 74

Haydon F S, (ed.) 1863 *Eulogium Historiarum, Chronicon a monachi malmesburiensi exoratum III*, Rolls Series

Herbert Sir T, 1815 *Memoirs of the last two years of the reign of Charles I*, London

Hewitt H J, 1958 *The Black Prince's Expedition*, (2004 reprint, Pen & Sword)

Hillier G, 1852 *A narrative of the attempted escapes of Charles the 1st from Carisbrooke Castle*, London

Hinds A B, 1912 *Calendar of State Papers and Manuscripts existing in the archives of Milan: 1*, HMSO London

Hinds A B, 1926 *Calendar of State Papers and Manuscripts relating to English Affairs existing in the archives and collections of Venice and other libraries of Northern Italy: 27 (1643–1647)*, HMSO London

Hinds A B, 1927 *Calendar of State Papers and Manuscripts relating to English Affairs existing in the archives and collections of Venice and other libraries of Northern Italy: 28 (1647–1652)*, HMSO London

Hinds A B, 1930 *Calendar of State Papers and Manuscripts relating to English Affairs existing in the archives and collections of Venice and other libraries of Northern Italy: 30 (1655–1656)*, HMSO London

Hinds A B, 1931 *Calendar of State Papers and Manuscripts relating to English Affairs existing in the archives and collections of Venice and other libraries of Northern Italy: 31 (1657–1659)*, HMSO London

Hingeston F C, (ed.) 1858 *Johannes Capgrave: De Illustribus Henricis*, Rolls Series

Hingeston F C, (ed.) 1858 *Chronicle of England by John Capgrave*, Rolls Series

Howlett R, (ed.) 1884 *Chronicles of the reigns of Stephen, Henry II and Richard I; I: Historia Rerum Anglicanum of William of Newburgh*, Rolls Series

Huehus G, (ed.) 1979 *Clarendon: selections from the history of the rebellion and The Life, by himself*, Oxford UP

Hutton R, 1989 *Charles II King of England, Scotland and Ireland*, Oxford Clarendon Press

Johnes, T. (transl.) 1845 *The chronicles of Enguerrand de Monstrelet; an account of the cruel civil wars between the houses of Orleans and Burgundy* (1807; 1845) 2 vols, London

Joinville J. (c1305 [1848]) 'Memoirs of Louis IX, King of France, commonly called St Louis', in Chronicles of the Crusades, Bohn's Historical Library; London

Jolliffe J, 1968 *Froissart's Chronicles*, London

Landon L, 1935 The Itinerary of King Richard I, *Pipe Roll Society* **51**, New Series 13

Leader, J D, 1880 *Mary Queen of Scots in Captivity: a narrative of events from January 1569 to December 1584, whilst George Earl of Shrewsbury was the guardian of the Scottish Queen*, Sheffield and London

Lettenhove Kervyn de (ed.) 1863–6 *Œuvres de Chastellain*, 8 Vols, Academie Royale de Belgique, Brussels

Luce S, 1862 *Chroniques des quatre premiers Valois*, Societé de l'histoire de France, Paris

Lumby J, (ed.) 1889–95 *Chronicle of Henry Knighton*, Rolls Series

Mackie, C, 1832 *The castles of Mary Queen of Scots*, Edinburgh

Mansel P, 1981 *Louis XVIII*, Bland and Briggs, London

McLeod E, 1969 *Charles of Orleans, Prince and Poet*, Chatto and Windus, London

Neilson N, (ed.) 1930 *Year Books of 10 Edward IV and 49 Henry VI (1470)*, Selden Society Yearbooks Series **47**

Ohler N, 2010 *The medieval traveller*, Boydell: Woodbridge

Power E, 1937 *Medieval people*, Pelican: London

Riley H T, (ed.) 1863 *Chronica monasterii S. Albani; Thome Walsingham, quondam monachi S. Albani; historia Anglicana; I: 1272–1381*, London

Riley H T, (ed.) 1864 *Chronica Monasterii S. Albani; Thome Walsingham, quondam monachi S. Albani: Historia Anglicana; II: 1381–1422*, London

Riley H T, (ed.) 1865 *Gesta Abbati monasterii Sancti Albani a Thomas Walsingham II*, Rolls Series

Rodney H, and Chapman J B W, (ed.) 1937 *Calendar of Inquisitions Miscellaneous (Chancery) III*, HMSO

Rose S, 2007 *The medieval sea*, Hambledon Continuum: London

Ross C, 1974 *Edward IV*, Book Club Associates, London

Rymer, T, 1705 *Foedera, Conventiones et Litterae*, 20 vols, London

Scafield, C-L, 1923 *Life and reign of Edward IV*; Longmans, London

Von Seggern H, 2003 *Herrschermedien in spätmittelalter Studien zur Infermatausüberlieferung im burgundischen Staat unter Karl dem Kühnen*, Kieler Historische Studien **41**, Sigmaringen

Society of Antiquaries, 1815 *Vetusta monumenta*: **IV**

Soden I, 2009 *Ranulf de Blondeville, the first English hero*, Amberley, Stroud

Smyth W H, 1851 Hartwell House, Buckinghamshire, *Gentleman's Magazine*, November 1851, 487–94

Starkey D, (ed.) 1990 *Rivals in Power: Lives and letters of the Great Tudor Dynasties*

Steinman G S, 1853 Memorials preserved at Bruges of King Charles the Second's residence in that city: referred to in a letter from G Steinman Steinman to Rt Hon Lord Braybrooke, *Archaeologia* **35**, 335–49

Stubbs W, (ed.) 1864 *Chronicles and memorials of the reign of Richard I: Itinerarum preregrinorum et gesta Regis Ricardi*, Rolls Series

Stubbs W, (ed.) 1865 *Chronicles and memorials of the reign of Richard I: Epistolae Cantuarienses 1187–1199*, Rolls Series

Stubbs W, (ed.) 1870 *Chronica Magistri Rogeri de Howedene, III*, Rolls Series

Thompson E M, (ed.) 1874 *Chronicon Anglicae 1328–1388 Auctore Monacho quodam Sancti Albani*, Rolls Series

Thompson E M, (ed.) *Correspondence of the family of Hatton 1601–1704: Vol I*, Camden Society

Tout T F, 1930 *Chapters in the administrative history of medieval England; the wardrobe, the chamber and the small seals 5*, Manchester UP

Twemlow J A, (ed.) 1909 *Calendar of Papal Registers; Papal Letters, VIII: 1427–47*, Rolls Series

Twemlow J A, (ed.) 1933 *Calendar of Papal Registers; Papal Letters, XII: 1458–71*, Rolls Series

Vaughan R, 1973 *Charles the Bold, London*

Whitaker K, 2003 *Mad Madge: Margaret Cavendish, Duchess of Newcastle, Royalist, Writer and Romantic*, London

Williams N, 1973 *The life and times of Henry VII, London*

Woolgar C M, 1999 *The Great Household in late medieval England*, Yale UP

Zacour N P, 1960 Talleyrand, the Cardinal of Périgord (1301–64), *American Philosophical Society* 50, 1–83

Zimmern H, 1891 *Hansa Towns*, London

INDEX